# 101
# WORD  GAMES

# 101
# WORD GAMES

## For Students of English as a Second or Foreign Language

### George P. McCallum

OXFORD UNIVERSITY PRESS

Oxford University Press
200 Madison Avenue, New York, NY 10016 USA

Walton Street, Oxford OX2 6DP England

OXFORD is a trademark of Oxford University Press.
Library of Congress Cataloging-in-Publication Data
McCallum, George P.
101 word games for students of English as a second or
foreign language.
Includes index.
1. English language—Study and teaching—Foreign
students.    2. Word game.    I. Title.
PE1128.A2M253      407      79-27525
ISBN 0-19-502742-6
Copyright © 1980 Oxford University Press.

Printing: 20  19  18  17  16  15  14

Printed in Hong Kong.

# CONTENTS

1081

92777

## Acknowledgments

Special mention should be made of the following persons who kindly contributed games and helpful suggestions to this collection: Richard Evans, George McCready, John Prindeville, Cynthia Schmidt, and Susan Pippitt Veguez.

G.P.M.

# INTRODUCTION

## Why use games in the English as a Second or Foreign Language classroom?

There are many valid reasons for using games in the language classroom, not least among them the sheer enjoyment of a moment of relaxation after some arduous drilling, or as a short respite after prolonged deskwork.

When one considers the importance of communicative competence in the target language, a major goal of all language acquisition, and the need for spontaneous and creative use of that language, one recognizes the significant role of word games in achieving these objectives. Students, in the informal atmosphere of game play, are less self-conscious and therefore more apt to experiment and freely participate in using the foreign language. In addition, games automatically stimulate student interest; a properly introduced game can be one of the highest motivating techniques.

Other reasons for including games in the language class are:

1. They focus student attention on specific structures, grammatical patterns, and vocabulary items.
2. They can function as reinforcement, review, and enrichment.
3. They involve equal participation from both slow and fast learners.
4. They can be adjusted to suit the individual ages and language levels of the students in the class.
5. They contribute to an atmosphere of healthy competition, providing an outlet for the creative use of natural language in a non-stressful situation.
6. They can be used in any language teaching situation and with any skill area whether reading, writing, speaking or listening.
7. They provide immediate feedback for the teacher.
8. They ensure maximum student participation for a minimum of teacher preparation.

Having justified the use of word games in the language class, accepting the fact that they provide not only a learning experience but an enjoyable one as well, we may then ask, when should a game be introduced? The logical time is toward the end of the hour—the "dessert" after the main course. However, there is no hidebound rule about this and whenever an instructor feels it is the appropriate moment for a more relaxing activity, that is the time for a game. All this is relative, of course, and it will be the good judgment of the instructor that determines the appropriate time.

## Choosing the Right Game

Which game should be played, once we've decided it is time for such an activity? Many factors enter into deciding the answer to this question:

1. the size of the class
2. whether it is a class of adults or one of children
3. the class level—elementary, intermediate, advanced
4. the structures being studied at the moment
5. the physical space you have to work with
6. the noise factor—will you disturb the classes around you?
7. the students' interests, in and out of class
8. the equipment and materials available
9. cultural considerations
10. the time available for a game

## Teacher Preparation

A game should be planned into the day's lesson right along with exercises, dialogs and reading practice. It should not be an afterthought.

Some games require the use of additional equipment or materials, such as flash cards, small, easily identifiable objects, a bean bag, stopwatch, blindfolds, or pencil and paper. These are noted at the top of each game. In most cases the equipment will already be available in the classroom. Where advance preparation is required for successful game play, it is recommended that the teacher assemble these materials prior to introducing the game.

Certainly the teacher should understand the game and how it is to be played before explaining the rules to the class. With certain games it might be wise to have two or three students give a short demonstration first, before the entire class participates. This will avoid confusion and cause the game to move along as smoothly as possible from the very beginning.

Once the rules are made clear, the teacher should see to it that they are adhered to. Changing rules in mid-game is bad strategy. If the rules as presented here seem too rigid for a particular group they can always be adjusted to suit the needs of that group, but this should be done before the game begins, not once it has started. No game has to be played exactly as presented; the teacher should always feel free to adapt it to the class. This is especially true when working with children. (See **Appendix:** *Games for Children*, 11 to 15.)

## Teacher as Facilitator

No matter how much the teacher actually participates in the game, he or she always remains in charge and keeps the situation under control. This is especially true when playing some of the physically active games and certainly when working with younger people. Certain games, by their very nature, require the teacher or someone in authority, such as a teacher's aid or even one of the students, to control the playing of the game once the rules are made clear. This can be done, and a relaxed atmosphere maintained, if the person in charge assumes the role of one more player who is guiding the game in the direction it should go, rather than dictating what the others should do. In other words, this person's positive attitude will be an important factor in deciding the success or failure of the game.

## Student Involvement

All of the class should be involved in one way or another. Choice of games will help here, of course, but it may be that for a specific reason—perhaps practice on a structure point—a teacher may want to use a game which is more effectively played by half a dozen students than by double or triple that number. Space permitting (not to mention noise level), there could be several groups around the room playing the same game at the same time. With other games, in which a few students only are required, the rest of the class could be judges, score-keepers or audience. Everyone should be made to feel he has some part in the game, even though for the moment it is a passive role. If space does not permit more than one small group to play at a time, then groups could take turns playing for a designated period of time. A panel of judges could, at the end of the hour, decide which group has played best.

## Do's and Don'ts

What do you do if you have chosen the perfect game for the perfect occasion and, lo and behold, it turns out to be a dud? You simply face up to the fact that today is not the day for that particular game (another day very likely will be) and as soon as possible you change activities. It may be, too, that an individual student does not feel like playing games that day, although the others do. Don't force him; he will neither enjoy nor benefit from the experience and will probably dampen the enjoyment of the others. Let him be an observer that day. No one should be forced to play games.

Looking on the brighter side, those times when you have great success with a game, and this is more usual, it is always wise to stop playing while the students are enjoying it and would prefer to continue. As far as repeating a popular game is concerned, discretion should be used. There is nothing wrong with playing a successful game on a later occasion but it is preferable to allow a decent interval of time before re-introducing it. Still better is the use of a different game the next time, though it could be a variation of one that students have especially enjoyed. *Buzz-Bizz* is a variation of *Buzz* that the class would undoubtedly enjoy even more than the original game, as it offers more of a challenge. This is also true of such games as *How's Your Vocabulary?* as opposed to *Catalogs*, and *Observe and Remember* as compared to *What Do You Remember?*

## Teamwork

A number of games require the dividing of the class into two teams. The teacher may want to do this differently each time—the boys against the girls, the right side of the room against the left side, row A versus row B, etc. However, there are some advantages to having the same teams for a month or even a full semester, especially in respect to the time it takes to divide the class each time a team game is played. Also, a certain team spirit develops which aids greatly in playing competitive games and promotes a free exchange of ideas both in- and outside of class. It is suggested that the teacher establish the teams, thus assuring that there will be an appropriate balance of faster students with slower ones in each group.

## Using this Book

The games in this collection are some of the many that can be played in the language class, and although these are designed for students learning English, many of them can easily be adapted for use with persons learning other languages. They have been categorized by chapter as follows:

1. Vocabulary Games
2. Number Games
3. Structure Games
4. Spelling Games
5. Conversation Games
6. Writing Games
7. Role Play and Dramatics

These are somewhat arbitrary classifications. Certain games, such as *Hidden Words*, found in the spelling section, is also a vocabulary game, and *Neither Yes nor No*, placed in the structure section, also gives practice in conversation. Thus, the teacher, seeking a good game for a specific purpose, perhaps structure practice, may find just what he or she wants among the writing games. It is recommended that the teacher check first the desired category, then the **Appendix** of *Games by Language Level*, and finally skim the **Objectives** of the appropriate games to find the most suitable selection for his or her class.

As will be noted throughout the collection, certain games lend themselves to homework assignments. Because of the enjoyable challenge of this type of activity, there should be no difficulty convincing the students to do their homework on such occasions. (See **Appendix:** *Games for Homework.*)

Certainly the teacher should feel free to take the raw material as presented here and make all the changes necessary for maximum effectiveness and fun with his or her class. It is also possible that a game cannot be played with a certain class because of the size of the group, their command of English, or the age of the students, but it will suggest a variation that will be successful. Teachers should feel free to experiment and use those games best suited to the individual needs of their students.

Each game is marked for **Language level:** elementary, intermediate, advanced, or all (meaning appropriate for all three levels). These markings are also flexible. An instructor may decide that his or her elementary class is quite capable of playing a game designed for intermediate and/or advanced students. Again, it is the teacher who decides which game is most applicable for any given class.

Where special equipment and materials are required for a game there is an indication: **Equipment and material.** A teacher's aid or one of the more responsible students could help gather or prepare those items required for the successful completion of a game.

The **Objective** of each game will be found directly under the title. This indicates the goal or specific language activity that the game introduces and reviews. In the Structure Games section, the principal structure or structures emphasized are also noted, in *italics*, within the general **Objective.**

The use of *It*, an American convention of game play, to designate the "performer" or focal player who begins the action of the game has been employed throughout this book. Very often it is this player who must leave the room; guess the secret word; question the other players; or generally initiate game play. Teachers may wish to select a more experienced student to be *It* for the opening round of play. Other students may then take turns being *It*, once the rules of the game have been established.

The masculine pronoun forms, *he, his,* and *him,* have been used here for the sake of simplicity and ease in reading. They should be understood to refer to both male and female students.

In her article, "Try One of My Games" (*English Teaching Forum,* May/June, 1970), Julia Dobson sums up the subject of games nicely: "I myself have found that a good language game is a wonderful way to break the routine of classroom drill, because it provides fun and relaxation while remaining very much within the framework of language learning—and may even reinforce that learning."

G. P. M.

*Madrid, Spain*
*April, 1980*

# 101
## WORD GAMES

# 1

## VOCABULARY GAMES

This section contains a variety of vocabulary games which give the students an opportunity to practice many of the high-frequency words and expressions they have learned.

# I Packed My Bag
# for Alaska

**Objective:** To increase the student's vocabulary by using a wide variety of common nouns and to provide practice with the indefinite articles, *a* and *an*.
**Language level:** all
**Equipment and material:** blackboard

This is a vocabulary building game that can be played successfully at any language level, though it is probably more fun for elementary and intermediate students than for advanced.

Begin the game by modeling the example sentence, "I packed my bag for Alaska and in mv bag I put *an apple*." The first student then repeats the model sentence and adds the name of an object that begins with the letter *B*. For example: "I packed my bag for Alaska and in my bag I put an apple and *a book*." The game is continued around the classroom with each student, in turn, repeating what has been said before and adding the name of a new object which begins with the next letter of the alphabet. Students should be encouraged to use their imaginations as the more ridiculous the objects, the more fun the game. If there are more than 26 students in the class, just begin the game again with the letter *A*. You may wish to write the names of objects beginning with the letters *Q*, *X*, and *Z* on the blackboard, or eliminate those letters from the game.

The first time this game is played you may wish to write, or have a student write, the names of all the objects on the blackboard as they are said. Once the students are familiar with the game they should be able to repeat the words they hear without referring to the blackboard.

To make this game more challenging to advanced classes, you might ask the students to provide an adjective before each object, such as, *a beautiful book, a clean coat, a dirty dress*, etc.

This game also provides practice with the indefinite articles, *a* and *an*. At a later date it could be played again, this time using plural nouns.

# Observe and Remember

**Objective:** To test the student's ability to observe and remember while reinforcing the vocabulary of high-frequency, common nouns.
**Language level:** all
**Equipment and material:** A variety of small, easily identifiable objects, as suggested below.

This is a good way to test a student's ability to observe and remember while building his vocabulary in English.

Before class, gather a wide selection of small, easily identifiable objects, such as a pencil, eraser, pen, wristwatch, teaspoon, notebook, keys, ruler, buttons, or whatever seems appropriate to the language level of the class. Place these objects on a desk or table at the front of the room.

Ask the students to come forward and look at the objects for a given length of time (no more than two minutes), and then have them return to their seats. Instruct the students to take out pencil and paper and write, in English, the names of as many objects as they can remember. At this point, cover the articles with a cloth or large piece of paper, thereby removing them from view. Allow approximately five minutes for the students to recall and write down the names of the things they have observed.

The number of items on the table, as well as the items themselves, should be appropriate to the language level of the class. About a dozen objects would be appropriate for an elementary class, fifteen to twenty for an intermediate group, and twenty-five to thirty for an advanced class.

When the students have finished writing, uncover the objects again and allow the students to come forward and check their work. Or, you may wish to hold up each individual item and have the students identify them in turn. The student with the most names, correctly spelled, wins.

*Other possible objects to use:*

| | |
|---|---|
| chalk | stapler |
| compass | paper clips |
| paper | envelope |
| scissors | tape |
| thread | can opener |
| magnet | toothbrush |
| glue | comb |

# What Do You Remember?

**Objective:** To test the student's ability to observe and remember while reinforcing the vocabulary of a wide variety of high-frequency, common nouns.
**Language level:** intermediate, advanced
**Equipment and material:** slide projector and slides or large wall charts

The basic concept of this game is similar to *Observe and Remember*, (p. 6). Students are provided with a variety of objects to observe, without being told why, after which they are asked to write down the names of as many objects as they can recall.

The difference between the two games is that instead of objects placed on a table, a colored slide or wall chart is used for displaying the objects which the students are to observe.

This has the advantage of providing a wider field of study, as well as increasing the challenge to the student, who may now have many more objects to identify.

After the students have compiled their lists, show the slide or picture again and have the students check their work as part of a whole-class activity.

# The A to Z Banquet

**Objective:** To practice the vocabulary of a wide variety of food items.

**Language level:** all

**Equipment and material:** blackboard

---

This is an excellent game for practicing the vocabulary of food items. The students may remain at their desks for this game or be arranged in a circle or semi-circle. Instruct the students to imagine that they have just been to a big banquet at which a variety of international foods were served. Going around the classroom, each student, in turn, is to tell what he ate at the banquet.

Begin by modeling the example sentence, "At the banquet I ate apple pie." The only rule is that each student must repeat all the previously mentioned food items and add a new dish beginning with the next letter of the alphabet.

The game proceeds as follows:

**Student 1:** At the banquet, I ate *apple pie*.

**Student 2:** At the banquet, I ate apple pie and *bacon*.

**Student 3:** At the banquet, I ate apple pie, bacon and *carrots*.

**Student 4:** At the banquet, I ate apple pie, bacon, carrots and *doughnuts*.

**Student 5:** At the banquet, I ate apple pie, bacon, carrots, doughnuts and *eggplant*.
(And so on.)

Eliminate such letters as X and Z and, according to the level of the class, any other letters for which it might be difficult to name a type of food.

For beginning level students, you may wish to hand out a prepared list of different foods and dishes. The first time the game is played, it is a good idea to write the food items on the blackboard, as they are said, to simplify the repetition.

To make the game move more rapidly, instead of repeating all the items previously mentioned, the student can add only the new food or dish, although the repetition does help the student learn new vocabulary.

# Animal Squares

**Objective:** To practice the vocabulary of the names of animals.
**Language level:** all
**Equipment and material:** prepared squares; pencils and erasers

This is a good game to assign as homework. Prepare enough copies of the *Animal Square* to allow each student to work independently. You may include the answers below, or wait until the following day in class to check the answers.

Hidden in the square are the names of twenty-five different animals. Ask the students to see how many names they can find and then have them draw a circle around each name. They may work both vertically and horizontally.

Encourage the students to find as many names as possible without checking the list below. Similar squares can be created with other categories: fruits, parts of the body, countries, etc.

Students may check their papers with those of their neighbors or one student may write the words on the blackboard as each student checks his own work. You may wish to bring in pictures of the less common animals for identification, particularly those not found in the student's native country.

*Animal Square:*

| L | I | O | N | X | E | S | F | K | C | A | T |
|---|---|---|---|---|---|---|---|---|---|---|---|
| O | M | X | I | B | L | O | R | D | K | Y | O |
| I | P | M | D | E | E | T | U | R | K | E | Y |
| R | A | O | Z | A | P | A | N | T | H | E | R |
| B | L | H | I | R | H | P | O | I | F | G | A |
| Z | A | D | O | G | A | E | T | G | O | A | T |
| W | R | E | K | N | N | P | T | E | X | Y | H |
| N | F | E | E | U | T | I | E | R | A | A | I |
| H | O | R | S | E | Z | G | R | M | L | K | E |
| O | B | U | F | F | A | L | O | W | O | L | F |
| B | A | B | O | O | N | W | S | H | E | E | P |
| X | L | E | I | U | T | M | O | O | S | E | N |

| | | | | |
|---|---|---|---|---|
| ape | deer | goat | otter | sheep |
| baboon | dog | gnu | ox | tiger |
| bear | elephant | horse | panther | turkey |
| buffalo | fox | impala | pig | wolf |
| cat | lion | moose | rat | yak |

12

# You'll Never Guess!

**Objective:** To encourage students to derive the meaning of new vocabulary items from contextual clues.
**Language level:** elementary and intermediate
**Equipment and material:** paper and pencil

Allow the students several minutes in which to write a brief description of some object for the others in the class to guess. Objects may be confined to a specific subject category, such as plants, animals, food or clothing, or a specific area, such as a classroom, bedroom, or schoolyard.

There should be four sentences in the description, beginning with the less obvious details and moving toward those that make it easier for the others to guess. Students may call out their answers as quickly as they think they know what the object is. The first student to guess correctly receives a score of one to four points.

A student receives four points if he guesses correctly after hearing the first sentence, three points after hearing the second sentence, two after the third and only one after the fourth sentence. At the end of the game the student with the most points is the winner.

*Option:* At the elementary level, you may wish to provide the vocabulary items on individual slips of paper. Each student is given an object to describe and the game proceeds as indicated above. This could also be assigned as homework.

*Examples:*

### Classroom Objects
1. It's big and usually black.
2. We use it every day.
3. There's one in almost every classroom.
4. The teacher writes on it.

   *Answer:* **blackboard**

## Classroom Objects

1. It's made of rubber.
2. It's very useful.
3. We need it when we make mistakes.
4. It is often found at the end of a pencil.

*Answer:*   **eraser**

# Seasons Greetings

**Objective:** To practice and identify vocabulary items associated with the four seasons.
**Language level:** elementary and intermediate

This game can be played in several different ways although the objective remains the same in each case.

*Option 1:* The teacher, or a student leader, calls out the name of something seasonal: a specific holiday, fruit, article of clothing, or activity, while the rest of the class calls out whichever season is associated with the object, *Spring, Summer, Fall* or *Winter.*

*Option 2:* The game can be played as directed above except that instead of shouting out the answers, the students raise their hands and the teacher calls on them, giving one point for each correct answer.

*Option 3:* This can be a team game with the questions being asked alternately of each team and one point given for each answer. The team with the most points at the end of the game wins.

*Warning:* There will be arguments as to whether a certain item is associated with *Spring* or *Summer,* another with *Fall* or *Winter.* You may wish to encourage an open discussion on these points but ultimately your decision should be final. Remind the students that seasonal associations refer to the place where the game is being played.

*Suggested list of seasonal items:*

| | | |
|---|---|---|
| strawberries | Thanksgiving Day | picnicking |
| Christmas | apples | Halloween |
| tulips | overcoat | watermelon |
| snow | roses | ice cream |
| swimsuit | falling leaves | ice-skating |
| Easter | camping | harvest time |
| air conditioning | skiing | valentines |

15

# Shopping Tour

**Objective:** To review the letters of the alphabet and to reinforce the vocabulary of high-frequency, common nouns.

**Language level:** intermediate

The students may sit at their desks or in a circle for this game. The first student begins the game by telling of a shopping tour he went on and the name of something he bought that begins with the letter *A*, such as *an armchair*.

The second student must name the armchair and add something beginning with the letter *B*. For example: "I went shopping and I bought an armchair and some *beer*." This procedure continues around the room and through the letters of the alphabet.

You may wish to suggest items beginning with the letters *Q*, *X*, and *Z*, or eliminate them from the game.

On another occasion the students could alter the procedure by adding an adjective to the object they mention. For example: "I went shopping and bought some *attractive ashtrays*."

# Alphabet Identification

**Objective:** To review the letters of the alphabet and to practice the names of people, places, and things.
**Language level:** intermediate

This game provides a quick review of the letters of the alphabet and should move rapidly around the classroom. Each student, in turn, gives imaginary information about him/herself following this format:

My name is＿＿＿＿＿＿.
My wife's/husband's name is＿＿＿＿＿＿.
We live in＿＿＿(city)＿＿.
And we sell＿＿＿＿＿＿.

The first student must fill in the blanks, orally or in writing, by providing words that begin with the letter A. The second student uses the letter B, the third student the letter C, and so on around the room. Such letters as Q, X, and Z, may be eliminated from the game.

*Examples:*

> My name is Anna.
> My husband's name is Andrew.
> We live in Atlanta.
> And we sell artichokes.

> My name is Bill.
> My wife's name is Barbara.
> We live in Boston.
> And we sell beans.

# What's Your Hobby?

**Objective:** To review the letters of the alphabet and to practice using the present continuous form of the verb with noun combinations.

**Language level:** intermediate

This is a fast-moving alphabet game. Each student is given two or three minutes, no more, to make up a hobby. It can be as ridiculous as he pleases but the first word must begin with the initial of his first name, and the second word with the initial of his last name.

Introduce the game by asking, "What's your hobby?" Each student will reply, in turn, "My name is _____ _____ and my hobby is _____ _____."

*Example:*

T:   What's your hobby?

S1:  My name is Mary Miller and my hobby is making money.

S2:  My name is David Hendricks and my hobby is digging holes.

S3:  My name is Billy Smith and my hobby is building skyscrapers.

S4:  My name is Tom Brown and my hobby is toasting bread.

*Variation:* Give the students the names of famous persons (living or dead), or let them choose their own, and ask what their hobbies are. The students respond using the name and initials of the famous person.

*Example:*

My name is Napoleon Bonaparte and my hobby is netting butterflies.

My name is Florence Nightingale and my hobby is finding needles.

# Color Call

**Objective:**   To review the names of colors and identify objects associated with those colors.
**Language level:**   intermediate and advanced
**Equipment and material:**   A bean bag or similar object for tossing, other than a ball.

This is a quick reaction game. It is especially good with young people, who get restless and need a release for their energy from time to time.

The players stand in a circle. One player has the bean bag. He throws it to another player in the circle, at the same time calling out a color.

The second player must catch the bean bag and, upon catching it, call out the name of something that is that color. He, in turn, tosses the bean bag to the next player, shouting out the name of a different color. The game proceeds as follows:

*Example:*
      **Player 1:**   Blue! (throwing the object to another player)
      **Player 2:**   Sky! (tosses object to a third player) Green!
      **Player 3:**   Grass! (tosses object to another player) Red!
      **Player 4:**   Tomato!

Colors may be repeated but the answers should be different. If one player gives *sky* for *blue,* then the next *blue* should be a different object of that color, such as *water.* For each error, a student receives a point against him. He also gets a point against him if he hesitates too long in answering. A player is eliminated from the game when he has three points against him. Whenever you wish to terminate the game, the player with the fewest (or no) points against him wins.

*Option:*   In a large class this could be a team game. The class could be divided into two teams which are lined up, facing each other.

Rather than tossing the bean bag at random, the players would throw it to the person opposite, going down the line, then starting back towards the front again. The team with the fewest errors at the end wins.

With intermediate students, you may want to write the names of some objects on the blackboard, though without the colors.

*Warning:* This is a noisy game and should be played outside, or in a room where the walls are thick enough so that the shouting won't disturb the class next door.

# I Like My Friend

**Objective:** To practice a wide variety of personal adjectives and review the first names of men and women.
**Language level:** intermediate and advanced
**Equipment and material:** blackboard

The rules of this game are simple. The first player begins by saying, "I like my friend with an A because her name is Alice and she is amiable" or, if referring to a man, ". . . because his name is Albert and he is amiable." The second player continues by saying, "I like my friend with a B because her/his name is Barbara/Bob and she/he is benevolent."

The students continue through the letters of the alphabet in this way. You may want to eliminate such letters Q, U, X, Y, and Z, as there are practically no names which begin with these letters.

For intermediate classes it would be a good idea to write a list of names and adjectives on the blackboard, although not in alphabetical order. The second time around, erase the names on the blackboard and go in a different order so that the student who had A or D or W the first time will have a different letter for which to find a name and adjective.

*Some names and adjectives:*

| | | |
|---|---|---|
| Alice | Albert | amiable |
| Barbara | Bob | benevolent |
| Carla | Charles | courageous |
| Dorothy | Donald | daring |
| Eva | Edward | efficient |
| Flora | Frank | faithful |
| Gloria | George | gentle |
| Helen | Henry | happy |
| Irene | Irving | intelligent |
| Jane | John | jovial |

21

| | | |
|---|---|---|
| Kathleen | Kenneth | kind |
| Laura | Leonard | loving |
| Mary | Michael | magnificent |
| Nancy | Norman | neat |
| Olive | Oscar | obedient |
| Patricia | Paul | polite |
| Rose | Ralph | respectable |
| Sarah | Sam | sweet |
| Trudy | Tom | tender |
| Virginia | Victor | virtuous |
| Wanda | William | wise |

# Word Matching

**Objective:** To practice high-frequency combinations of synonyms and antonyms.
**Language level:** intermediate and advanced
**Equipment and material:** pencil and paper

For some reason we have the habit of thinking of objects in pairs; we hear one word and immediately think of another. This association is significant to psychologists. It is also interesting to teachers of English as a Second or Foreign Language and can be entertaining as well as useful.

Prepare a list of items for which there are many associations. You may wish to use things of a similar type, synonyms, or opposites, antonyms, or half of an easily identifiable pair. Many combinations are possible.

Begin the game by reading the first half of the list of words. The students should write the second word as quickly as they can, putting down the first association that comes to mind. Afterwards, re-read your list of pairs and have the students check to see how close they have come to the conventional associations. Make it a point to tell the students that there are no right or wrong associations in this game; therefore there can be no winner. A good discussion often results.

*Example associations:*

| | | | |
|---|---|---|---|
| hot—cold | rich—poor | wet—dry | pass—fail |
| big—little | right—wrong | noisy—quiet | hungry—thirsty |
| tall—short | happy—sad | girl—boy | sharp—dull |
| fat—thin | sick—well | aunt—uncle | fast—slow |
| knife—fork | high—low | sell—buy | clean—dirty |

# How's Your Vocabulary?

**Objective:** To test the student's active vocabulary.
**Language level:** intermediate and advanced
**Equipment and material:** pencil and paper; blackboard

Make sure each student has a pencil and paper before beginning this game. When the class is ready, write one letter of the alphabet on the blackboard, and have the students write down all the words they can think of that begin with that letter.

No more than two minutes should be allowed for the students to write. At the end of two minutes, call "Time" and have the students count their words. The one with the most words wins, though they must be bona fide words from the dictionary.

With advanced students the words should be correctly spelled; with intermediate students you may wish to allow a half point for words incorrectly spelled. It is advisable to restrict the inclusion of slang, abbreviations and proper names.

# Key Word

**Objective:** To reinforce high-frequency vocabulary items by providing common associations for each item.
**Language level:** high intermediate and advanced
**Equipment and material:** prepared flash cards

In this game the class is divided into two teams and two students are selected to represent each team. These four players go to the front of the room and sit in previously arranged chairs: one member of each team facing forward, the other two players facing the class.

As the game begins the teacher, or a student assistant who does not belong to either team, holds up a card with a word printed on it. The entire class and the two players facing forward can see the word, but the two students facing the class cannot see it. The object of the game is for the player who sees the word to give one-word clues to his partner, so that the partner may try and guess the word; the teams alternate back and forth after each attempt to guess the word. The game proceeds as follows:

*Example:*
(Teacher or student assistant holds up the word *shoe*.)

> **Team A, S1:** (seeing the word) foot
> **Team A, S2:** walk
> **Team B, S1:** (seeing the word) wear
> **Team B, S2:** stocking
> **Team A, S1:** leather
> **Team A, S2:** shoe (wins the round)

Each team has five opportunities to guess the word. If they cannot discover what the word is in that time, they go on to the next item. The team that guesses the word gets one point. Five words are presented in this way and then the two players of each team change positions, so that the partner previously giving the clues now tries to guess the words.

In order to have more students participate, you may wish to have new pairs come to the front of the room after each five words, rather than have the same two players change places. This will depend on the size of the class, the language level of the students and the time available.

The team with the most points at the end of the game is the winner. There is no set time for guessing but if after some ten seconds a player cannot guess the word, you should indicate that the other team now has its turn; otherwise the game slows down and the students become restless.

# Tessie Billings

**Objective:** To practice the third person singular of verbs, in both the affirmative and negative forms, as well as *Yes/No questions* with *do*.

**Language level:** intermediate and advanced

As this is a guessing game it would be advisable to let two students know the secret of the game beforehand.

Begin the game with the two informed students, while the rest of the class listens. The other students should be invited to participate as soon as they think they have discovered how the game is played.

The two informed players begin the game as follows:

**Player 1:** Tessie loves coffee but hates tea.

**Player 2:** Tessie prefers rubber gloves to leather ones.

**Player 1:** Tessie likes bees but she doesn't like honey.

**Player 2:** Tessie's favorite state is Tennessee but she doesn't like Georgia.

Little by little it should become evident to the other students that Tessie only likes things spelled with double letters and they can begin asking such questions as the following:

**Player 3:** Does Tessie like butter?

**Player 1:** Yes, but she can't stand bread.

**Player 4:** Does Tessie like milk?

**Player 2:** No, she doesn't, but she loves cheese.

As the rest of the class catches on, they too can provide yes/no answers to the questions.

# Vegetables and Things

**Objective:** To provide practice in using the dictionary to expand the student's recognition vocabulary of vegetables, fruits, flowers and animals.

**Language level:** intermediate and advanced

**Equipment and material:** dictionaries; paper and pencil

Have each student draw a square, divided into sixteen boxes, as illustrated below. A person's name, either male or female (consisting of four letters), is written across the top, one letter for each box. The entire class uses the same name at the same time. Down the left side, coinciding with each of the squares, are four categories: *vegetables, fruits, flowers,* and *animals.*

The students then fill in the sixteen boxes with words that begin with the letter at the top of the column, and are in the class of nouns indicated at the left.

*Example:*

|  | C | O | R | A |
|---|---|---|---|---|
| **Vegetables** | cauli-flower | okra | radish | artichoke |
| **Fruits** | cherry | orange | raspberry | apple |
| **Flowers** | carnation | oleander | rose | azalea |
| **Animals** | cat | otter | rat | ape |

Four points are scored for each entry *not* selected by anyone else and one point for each entry used by other students. The student, or student team, with the most points is the winner. This is an ideal homework exercise, as well as dictionary practice.

*Option:* For lower level students, you may wish to draw a large square on the blackboard, and have the whole class participate in filling in the boxes.

# In the Dark

**Objective:** To provide practice in identifying and recording the names of a variety of common objects.
**Language level:** all
**Equipment and material:** A variety of small objects; pencil and paper; blindfolds.

Before class, collect ten or twelve small objects, the names of which should be known to the class. For elementary classes, such objects as a *book*, a *pencil*, a *watch*, and a *shoe* might be used. For intermediate students, a *ring*, a *pair of glasses*, a *potato*, and a *light bulb* could be included. Advanced students should be able to identify such articles as a *candlestick*, a *pocket calculator*, a *cassette tape*, and a *salt shaker*. You, the teacher, will be aware of what vocabulary items your students have learned and choose accordingly.

Each student will be blindfolded and will have a pencil and piece of paper on which to write the names of the articles as they are passed around from one to another. The students are not to say the names out loud. After the ten or twelve articles have been passed around and their names written down, the blindfolds are removed. You then hold up each article (in the same order that it was passed around) and name it. The students check their lists as you do so. Of course it may be a bit difficult, because of the blindfolds, for them to write well but as they only have to write one word at a time they should be able to read their own writing without too much difficulty. The student with the most correct list of names is the winner.

In a large class this could be a small group activity, with several groups working at the same time. If so, then one student in each group could act as teacher, passing and collecting the objects to be guessed.

# Teakettle

**Objective:** To identify and practice the differences in spelling and meaning of high-frequency homonyms.
**Language level:** intermediate and advanced
**Equipment and material:** paper and pencil

This is a game of homonyms: words that sound alike but have different meanings and are usually spelled differently.

Have one student leave the room. The other students in the class agree on a pair of homonyms, *right* and *write*, for example. Each student thinks of a different sentence involving both words. It isn't important for the sentences to make too much sense but they must accurately illustrate the distinct meaning of the homonym. Intermediate students should be permitted to write down their sentences.

The missing student, *It,* is then brought back into the classroom and asked to try and guess the selected pair of homonyms. The rest of the students, in turn, read their sentences aloud, substituting the word *teakettle* for the words to be guessed.

Assuming that *right* and *write* are the words, some of the sentences could be:

I always *teakettle* (write) with my *teakettle* (right) hand.

I insist on my *teakettle* (right) to *teakettle* (write) the President.

Please *teakettle* (write) that sentence again; it isn't *teakettle* (right).

When *It* guesses the words being substituted for by *teakettle,* the student whose sentence has given him the clue becomes *It* and leaves the room. A new pair of homonyms is then selected and the game begins again.

# Sally Smith

**Objective:** To provide practice with adjective-noun combinations covering a broad range of vocabulary items.
**Language level:** intermediate and advanced
**Equipment and material:** paper and pencil

In this game the students have to come up with adjectives and nouns that begin with the letter S. To save time and make the game move more rapidly, at least with the intermediate students, you may want to give the class a few minutes—two or three, no more—to write down their ideas, then go around the class having them read aloud what they have written. The idea is that *Sally Smith* only likes things that begin with the letter S.

*Example:*

      Sally likes silk stockings.
      Sally likes soft scarves.
      Sally likes strawberry shortcake.

*Variations:*

Instead of *Sally* the name could be *Margaret*.

      Margaret likes mysterious men.
      Margaret likes messy macaroni.

A man's name, such as *Bob*, could also be used.

      Bob likes big buildings.
      Bob likes bouncing balls.

Another variation is to assign each student, or several small teams of students, a different name to work with and set a time limit, asking them to come up with as many adjective-noun combinations as possible in that time.

# Catalogs

**Objective:** To test and reinforce the student's active vocabulary within a broad range of subject categories.
**Language level:** intermediate and advanced
**Equipment and material:** paper and pencil; blackboard

Begin the game by writing a letter of the alphabet on the blackboard. Within a given length of time the students are to compile a list of the names of all the objects in the room which begin with that letter.

For advanced students, no more than two minutes should be given; for intermediate students, no more than four minutes. The student with the longest, and most accurate, list is the winner.

Later this game can move out of the classroom, into the world, becoming a general knowledge test. Within the given time limit the students could create catalogs of the following:

1. names of different kinds of fruit
2. well-known authors
3. famous composers
4. important rivers of the world
5. names of flowers
6. games and sporting events
7. different kinds of vegetables
8. articles of clothing worn by men and women
9. home furnishings
10. parts of the body

It is generally a good idea to prepare a list of probable student responses before class, to avoid selecting a category and letter for which there are few or difficult selections.

# Words from Words

**Objective:**  To provide a fast-paced review, either orally or in writing, of a broad selection of vocabulary items.
**Language level:**  intermediate and advanced
**Equipment and material:**  paper and pencil

Begin the game by giving each of the students, in turn, a word. He or she takes the first letter of the word and, in a designated time, gives as many words beginning with that letter as possible. About two minutes is appropriate for an intermediate group; one minute for advanced classes.

*Example:*
**Teacher:**  book
**Student:**  bring, bottle, buy, boy, Brazil, Bob, building, bus. . . .

The student who names the most words in the allotted time is the winner.

*Option 1:*  This can also be a written game, with all of the students in the class writing down as many words as they can in the time allotted. The student with the longest, and most accurate, list wins.

*Option 2:*  It is also possible to make a team game out of this, by dividing the class into two teams, and conducting the game in the manner of a spelling bee, calling on the members of each team alternately. If played in this manner, each student should be allowed no more than one minute in which to respond, otherwise the game goes on too long. In this version of the game, one point is given for each correct word and the team with the most cumulative points at the end of the game wins.

# Simple and Compound

**Objective:** To provide practice with prefixes and suffixes.
**Language level:** advanced
**Equipment and material:** pencil and paper

Write a word, a prefix or a suffix on the blackboard. Give the students five minutes to make a list of simple or compound words that incorporate the word or affix. At the end of the game the student with the longest list wins.

This could also be a small group activity, with six or seven students working together. The group with the most words wins.

In addition to such prefixes as *un*, *dis* and *de*, and such suffixes as *–tion*, *–ment* and *–ious*, the words *self*, *head*, *heart*, and *strong* are excellent base words.

*Example:*

| | |
|---|---|
| **self** (written on the blackboard) | self-contained |
| selfish | self-supporting |
| selfless | self-respect |
| self-made | myself |
| self-confident | yourself |
| self-conscious | himself |
| self-righteous | herself |
| self-sufficient | itself |

# Dictionary Dilemma

**Objective:** To familiarize students with dictionary format and to allow them to practice using the dictionary to discover the meaning of unfamiliar vocabulary items.
**Language level:** advanced
**Equipment and material:** A dictionary for each student; paper and pencil.

---

Before class, select a word from the dictionary that is outside the students' present vocabulary, something quite obscure and thought provoking. In class, direct the students to take out paper and pencil, and to have their dictionaries handy. Then pronounce the word but do not write it on the blackboard. The students copy down what they think they heard. They then proceed to write a definition of the word, following as much as possible the format of a dictionary: origin, part of speech, definition, synonyms, and an example sentence containing the word. You will also prepare a slip of paper, although giving the correct definition, etc., according to the dictionary.

When everyone has written out his definition (preferably on the same size pieces of paper so that yours will be exactly like the others), collect the papers, shuffle them and hand them out again. Each student then reads aloud from the paper which has just been given to him. At the end the students vote on the definition they believe to be the correct one. The definition receiving the most votes wins.

When the voting is over, read the correct version aloud, which may or may not have been the winner. At this point it is helpful for the students themselves to check the word in the dictionary.

A good discussion often results from this game. It is very helpful in familiarizing the students with the dictionary and its uses.

A sample list of words from the dictionary which are appropriate for this game are:

| pard | effrontery | quietus | vie | lag | adjure |
|------|-----------|---------|-----|-----|--------|
| bleak | salver | wraith | husk | captious | chaff |

35

# Name Game

**Objective:** To provide vocabulary practice using specific subject and letter categories in a fast-recall game.
**Language level:** advanced

This is a team game and might, in the excitement, become a bit noisy as the students are required to shout out answers as rapidly as possible. The teacher watches the time and a reliable student assistant keeps score.

Select a list of subject categories paired with a letter of the alphabet. Prepare individual slips of paper, indicating a separate category and letter on each. Have the first player or captain of Team A select a slip, calling out the category and letter to which Team B will respond. The members of Team B name as many things within the category, that begin with that letter, as possible. They do not wait for turns but shout out the answers as quickly as they can. You may, with a stopwatch, note the time, usually one minute, and have a student note the number of answers given by Team B in that time.

Then Team B gives Team A a category and a letter and they have their minute to provide as many items as possible within the selected category that begin with that letter. The team that has the longest list of items at the end of the game wins.

*Example:*

> **Team A, Leader:** Flowers. The letter *D*.
> **Team B:** Daffodil! Daisy! Dogwood! Dandelion! Dahlia!
> **Teacher:** Time!
> **Team B, Leader:** Countries. The letter *B*.
> **Team A:** Bolivia! Belgium! Bulgaria! Brazil!

# Earth, Air, Fire, and Water

**Objective:** To practice the names of plants and animals and to classify these items according to the environment in which they are most commonly found.

**Language level:** advanced

**Equipment and material:** bean bag

The class should be divided into two teams for this game and arranged to sit facing each other.

Each side has a leader, one of whom will be handed a bean bag, or other object for tossing. He or she will begin the game by tossing the object to a player on the opposite side, at the same time calling out, *Earth, Air, Fire,* or *Water*. The player receiving the object must, before the thrower counts to ten, call out the name of some plant or animal that lives in the air, on the earth, or in the water. If the word *Fire* is called out the person to whom the object is tossed must remain silent.

A player who receives the object but cannot think of a suitable answer may toss it to another member of his own team, but the latter must then reply before the count of ten is reached by the first thrower on the opposite team. A player who on two occasions fails to answer or who calls out of turn, has to leave the game.

The call of *Earth, Air, Fire,* or *Water* is alternately made by the leaders of the two teams and the side which first eliminates all of its opponents, or has the most players remaining in the game, within the allotted time, wins.

*Examples:*

**Earth:**  dog, cat, horse, elephant, bear, camel, grass, trees, vegetables, fruit trees, flowers

**Air:**  eagle, sparrow, robin, seagull, hawk, owl, pigeon, crow, canary, dove, parrot

**Water:**  dolphin, whale, shark, octopus, lobster, salmon, tuna, eel

# 2

---

# NUMBER GAMES

One of the first things that students learn to do is count, which means they are able to play simple, and enjoyable, number games very early in their language learning experience.

Buzz
Buzz-Bizz
Take a Number
Numbered Chairs
Numbers Quiz
The Power of Concentration

# Buzz

**Objective:** To provide counting practice.
**Language level:** elementary and intermediate

This is a counting game that can be played as soon as the students learn to count to 100 in English.

Any number can be chosen as the *buzz* number, but perhaps the first time around, at least with elementary students, it should be an easy one, such as 5.

The game proceeds as follows: The first student begins by saying, "one," the second student, "two," the third student, "three," the fourth student, "four," but the fifth student, instead of saying "five," says "*buzz*." The counting continues around the class, as rapidly as possible to add excitement to the game, and the student who would otherwise say "ten" will say "*buzz*." All multiples of the number 5 become *buzz*. If a student says the number rather than the word *buzz* he is out of the game. The last remaining student is the winner.

If another number is chosen, such as 3, then, in addition to all multiples of that number, all other numbers which contain a 3, such as 13 and 23 also become *buzz*. When the game reaches 30 the next ten numbers are all *buzz*, and students will have to keep on their toes to discover where *buzz* stops and 40 begins.

This is a game that can be repeated more than once but it is a good idea to use a different number—and a more difficult one—as *buzz* each time.

# Buzz-Bizz

**Objective:**   To provide counting practice.
**Language level:**   elementary and intermediate

This is a variation on *Buzz* and can be played soon after the students have mastered the original game. Students enjoy the added challenge of *Buzz-Bizz*.

The basic rules are the same as for *Buzz*, in that a number, such as 3, will be chosen for *buzz*. For all multiples and other numbers containing a 3 the students will say *buzz*. In addition, another number, perhaps 7, will become *bizz*. Each time a multiple or number containing a 7 comes up the student must say *bizz*. When a student comes to 21, he must say *buzz-bizz*, as both 3 and 7 are involved.

This game should move quickly. When a student makes a mistake by saying the number rather than *buzz* or *bizz* he is out of the game.

# Take a Number

**Objective:** To improve listening comprehension skills and test the student's ability to follow directions.
**Language level:** all
**Equipment and material:** paper and pencil

In this game the students must follow your directions, exactly as stated, in order to successfully complete the activity.

Begin by telling the class, "Take a number, any number. Double it. Add_____(any *even* number you, the teacher, select). Divide the resulting number in half. Subtract_____(half the even number you added in step 3). The answer, if you have followed directions correctly, will be the number you originally thought of."

After playing this as a whole class activity a couple of times, just enough to make sure the students understand, arrange them in pairs and let them tell each other, "Take a number."

*Examples:*

| Take a number: | 8 | Take a number: | 14 |
|---|---|---|---|
| Double it: | 16 | Double it: | 28 |
| Add 4: | 20 | Add 6: | 34 |
| Divide resulting number in half: | 10 | Divide resulting number in half: | 17 |
| Subtract 2: | 8 | Subtract 3: | 14 |

| | |
|---|---|
| Take a number: | 227 |
| Double it: | 454 |
| Add 102: | 556 |
| Divide resulting number in half: | 278 |
| Subtract 51: | 227 |

# Numbered Chairs

**Objective:** To improve listening comprehension skills by using a fast-reaction number game.

**Language level:** all

This is a game of concentration, although the only things the students have to remember are as many numbers as there are players in the game.

For this game the players should sit in a row or semi-circle. Each player has a number, although that number really belongs to the chair. In other words, the player has that particular number as long as he remains in that chair; each time he moves he gets a new number—the one belonging to the new chair.

Let's assume there are twelve players seated in a semi-circle. The first player calls out a number, any one up to twelve. For example, he calls 7. The student sitting in chair number 7 then calls out another number, for example 5, and number 5 calls out yet another number. As soon as a player hears his number called he immediately says a different number, though always within the range of numbers for which there are players in the game, and never his own number.

If a player repeats his own number or one beyond the number of players in the game, or if he hesitates too long in answering, he must go to the end of the row and take the last seat, becoming number 12, or whatever the final number is. This means that all the players up to his number must move up one seat and thus have a new number.

For example: If the one who has made a mistake is number 6, then everybody from 7 through 12 moves up one chair; those seated in chairs 1 through 5 do not move. All these players, 7 to 12, must now forget their old numbers and concentrate on their new ones. This is where the challenge of concentration comes in, especially if the game has gone on for a while without a change and the students have become used to being a certain number.

There is no winner for this game but students enjoy it and it can go on for a considerable length of time without becoming a bore. It can be played successfully at all levels.

# Numbers Quiz

**Objective:** To practice using numbers through a question and response activity.

**Language level:** intermediate and advanced

**Equipment and material:** flash cards with numbers

All the questions asked in this number game are answered by a single number or combination of numbers. To begin the game, divide the class into two teams and give each team member a card with one number on it, 0 through 9.

You then ask a series of questions, directing one question to each team, in turn. When the question is asked, the students with the appropriately numbered flash cards step forward as quickly as possible, without speaking, and arrange themselves to form the correct answer. In preparing the questions, be certain that there are a sufficient quantity of cards with numbers to answer all of the questions asked. For example, if one of the questions is, "When was the American Declaration of Independence signed?" there would have to be two 7's for the students to be able to form the correct answer, 1776.

Where classes are small, it may be necessary for students to have more than one card. For larger groups, the numbers could run beyond 9. Much depends on the questions to be asked.

If the answer requires more than one number, as in a date, for example, the students with the necessary numbers to form the date must step forward and, as quickly as possible, arrange themselves in order: 1–4–9–2.

This is an excellent game to play when studying weights and measures.

| *Sample questions:* | *Answers:* |
|---|---|
| 1. How many inches in a foot? | (12) |
| 2. How many feet in a yard? | (3) |
| 3. How many feet in a mile? | (5,280) |

4. How many ounces in a pound? (16)
5. How many pounds in a ton? (2,000)
6. How many pints in a quart? (2)
7. How many quarts in a gallon? (4)
8. What is normal body temperature, centigrade? (37)
9. When was the American Declaration of Independence signed? (1776)
10. On what day in December does Christmas fall? (25)

# The Power of Concentration

**Objective:**  To improve listening comprehension skills by following directions, exactly as stated, to solve a numerical problem.
**Language level:**  advanced
**Equipment and material:**  pencil and paper

This is a difficult game and requires complete concentration.

Begin by reading the following instructions, repeating them as many times as is necessary. Inform the students that they must do exactly as they are told. If they make one minor mistake everything else will also be wrong.

*Instructions:*
1. Write the number that represents one-fourth of a century. (25)
2. Under this number write the number of quarters in a dollar. (4)
3. Do *not* follow the next instruction if the city of Chicago is in the state of California. (It is not.)
4. Under the number of quarters in a dollar write the number of nickels in a quarter. (5) If this is larger than the number just above it, write the number of pennies in a dime (10) *to the right* of the total of the last two numbers (9), which you place under the number of nickels in a quarter.
5. Now cross out the number of pennies in a dime, if you have written it, but only if the sum of the first two numbers you wrote on your paper is more than ten. (It is.)
6. Add *all* the numbers you have written down, including the one you may have crossed out. (25, 4, 5, 10, 9 = 53)
7. Multiply the total by two. (106) This is known as the total number.
8. If the city of San Francisco is west of the city of Chicago, subtract 6 from the total number. (100)
9. Divide the resulting number by the number of quarts in a gallon. (4)

10. The resulting number should now be the number of pennies in a quarter. (25) It is also the answer to the first question.

*Answer:*

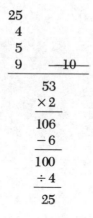

$$25$$
$$4$$
$$5$$
$$9 \quad \cancel{10}$$
___
$$53$$
$$\times 2$$
___
$$106$$
$$-6$$
___
$$100$$
$$\div 4$$
___
$$25$$

49

# 3

## STRUCTURE GAMES

Perhaps the most instructive language learning games are those that emphasize specific grammatical structures. They not only practice basic structures but do so in a pleasant, easy way that allows the students to forget they are drilling grammar and to concentrate on having fun.

The following games are concerned with *Yes/No questions*, *Wh- questions*, *tag questions*, the *conditional*, the *comparative* and *superlative*, *adverbs*, *modals*, *demonstratives*, *verb forms*, and the *future* with *going to*.

There are also many games that give the students practice in question formation, something that is often neglected in the formal class where the teacher does most of the asking and the students only respond.

Bananas

Big, Bigger, Biggest

This or That

Roll the Blocks

Teapot

Identification

I'm Going to Take a Trip

First Guess

Neither Yes nor No

Thousand Dollars

News Reporter

Twenty Questions

Secret Formula

Where, When, and How?

Who Am I?

Questions Only, Please

Answer My Question

Nonsense

Tell the Truth

Things Could Be Different

Turn Left, Turn Right

# Bananas

**Objective:** To practice *Wh-question* formation.
**Language level:** all

One player is chosen to be *It*. All of the other players ask him a wide variety of *Wh-questions* of a personal nature. He makes one reply to all their questions: *Bananas*. The aim of the game is to make *It* laugh or smile, and when he does, someone else, the person who has caused him to laugh, takes his place.

The questions should be such as to make the answer as ridiculous as possible. In this game *Yes/No questions* are not permitted to be asked, only *Wh- questions*.

As this is a popular game, students will probably want to play it again. Rather than *bananas* a different word could be substituted—*spaghetti, onions,* or *spinach,* would also work well.

*Example:*
**Player 1:**   What do you like best in the world?
**It:**   Bananas.
**Player 2:**   What do you wash your face with every morning?
**It:**   Bananas.
**Player 3:**   What are you going to wear to Mary's party?
**It:**   Bananas.
**Player 4:**   What are you going to name your new baby?
**It:**   Bananas. (This causes *It* to laugh, which means that the person who made him or her laugh will now be *It*.)

# Big, Bigger, Biggest

**Objective:**  To practice the *comparative* and *superlative* forms.
**Language level:**  elementary
**Equipment and material:**  blackboard

This is a good game for all ages but it works especially well with young people. The class should be divided into two teams and the score kept on the blackboard by the teacher.

A player from one team stands up and says, "I have the longest hair in the class." If a member of the opposing team disagrees, he or she stands up and says, "My hair is longer than your hair." If there is any question about it, the two should be brought to the front of the room and their hair measured. The student with the longest hair gets a point for his or her team. The team with the most points at the end of the game wins.

If it seems advisable, you may, before the game begins, make suggestions about things that can be compared and in what ways.

*Example topics:*

> height—tall, taller, tallest
> shoe size—big, bigger, biggest
> age—old, older, oldest
> age—young, younger, youngest

54

# This or That

**Objective:** To practice the *demonstratives, this/that,* and to provide an opportunity for *Yes/No question* formation.
**Language level:** elementary and intermediate

Two students are told the secret of the game, but in such a way (before class) that the other students won't suspect that there is a trick to it. One of them is selected to be *It* and leaves the room. The other student tells the class to pick an object in the room which *It* will have to guess.

*It* returns to the room and the first student begins asking questions and pointing at various objects in the room. He will ask, "Is it this table?" *It* will answer "No," until the first student asks, "Is it that picture?" at which time *It* answers, "Yes." The trick of the game is that when the questioner asks, "Is it *that?*" instead of "Is it *this?*" the other student, *It,* knowing the secret, replies "Yes." Of course, this game can only be played once this way, but the secret word can be changed from time to time and thus the game can be repeated.

*Example:*

> **Student 1:** (pointing) Is it this book?
> **It:** No, it isn't.
> **Student 1:** Is it this chair?
> **It:** No, it isn't.
> **Student 1:** Is it this piece of chalk?
> **It:** No, it isn't the chalk.
> **Student 1:** Is it that desk?
> **It:** Yes, it's the desk.

If one of the other students in the class thinks he has learned the code and wants to try, he should be given the opportunity to do so. If he guesses correctly, he wins. Another student may then try to break the code. The game continues until the majority of the students have guessed the trick, or you feel it is time to reveal the secret. One of the students who guessed correctly should then explain the trick to the rest of the class.

# Roll the Blocks

**Objective:** To provide practice in *sentence formation*.
**Language level:** elementary
**Equipment and material:** two wooden blocks

Paste selected common nouns on the six sides of one block; on the other block paste verbs, pronouns, and articles. As this is a good game to play in small groups, you may want to prepare several sets of blocks in this way.

In turn, the students roll the blocks, as they would dice, and try to make sentences out of the words that appear on top. For example, the words *he* and *door* may turn up. The student is free to make up any sentence he wishes using these two words: "He opened the door." "He closed the door." "He went to the door." There are various possibilities, much depending on the vocabulary and structures at the student's command.

In preparing the blocks you should have in mind a quantity of possible word combinations that might result from the rolling of the blocks. On one block you might have: *door, window, box, book, bag,* and *drawer*. On the other could be: *open, close, he, she, the, a*.

If this is played in small groups, you could give the signal to begin and each group could begin rolling the blocks and making up sentences, one by one. A recording secretary for each group could write down each sentence as it is said aloud. The first group to finish with the most correct sentences wins.

# Teapot

**Objective:** To practice using a wide variety of *verbs* by guessing each item through the use of *Yes/No questions*.
**Language level:** elementary and intermediate

One of the students is chosen to be *It* and is sent out of the room. The other students agree on a verb: to study, to run, to eat, etc. Simple verbs should be chosen at first.

*It* returns to the classroom and goes around the group asking *Yes/No questions*, using the word *teapot* to take the place of the unknown verb. For example, if the verb to be guessed is *run* he may ask such questions as:

| | |
|---|---|
| **It:** | Do I *teapot* with my hands? |
| **S1:** | No. |
| **It:** | Do I *teapot* with my eyes? |
| **S2:** | No. |
| **It:** | Do I *teapot* with my feet? |
| **S3:** | Yes. |
| **It:** | Is *teapotting* walking? |
| **S4:** | No. |
| **It:** | Is it running? |
| **S5:** | Yes. |

# Identification

**Objective:** To provide practice in *Yes/No questions* and answers.
**Language level:** elementary and intermediate

One student is told the secret of the game and sent out of the room. The remaining students select an object in the room and the student who is *It* returns. The teacher begins asking him a series of questions, each prefaced with "Is it. . . ?" to which *It* answers "No," until the teacher comes to the selected object, at which time he asks, *"Tell me,* is it. . . ?" The clue, of course, is *"Tell me,* is it. . . ?" That is, the teacher will ask questions beginning with "Is it. . . ?" until he decides it is time to ask about the correct object, and begins his question with, *"Tell me. . ."* The teacher should be casual in saying this or too many students will discover the trick early in the game.

After the first time around, ask for volunteers to be *It*, and the student who has just guessed the right answer should now ask the questions. The volunteers, of course, are not told the code but must discover it for themselves.

# I'm Going to Take a Trip

**Objective:** To provide practice in *What questions* and statements with the *future be + going to*.
**Language level:** intermediate
**Equipment and material:** blackboard

In this game the students may remain seated at their desks. The first student begins the game by saying, "I'm going to take a trip to Africa. What am I going to do there?" The second student must answer the question with a verb and noun which begins with the same letter as the name of the place previously stated. For example: "You're going to *a*nswer *a*dvertisements in *A*frica."

The second student then asks a question concerning a place beginning with the letter *B*. For example, "I'm going to take a trip to Brazil. What am I going to do there?" The third student replies, "You're going to buy bananas in Brazil." He then asks a question with the letter *C*, to which the fourth student responds, and so on around the room.

If the teacher prefers, the students may choose any letter they wish, not necessarily in alphabetical order. However, they should be warned not to repeat a place name that has been given before.

The first time the game is played the teacher should write suggestions on the blackboard—a list of place names, verbs, and nouns.

# First Guess

**Objective:** To provide practice in *Yes/No question* formation.
**Language level:** intermediate

---

Divide the class into several groups of from five to ten students each, depending upon the size of the class. Each group chooses an object; the more difficult it is to guess the better. A representative is also selected from each group.

When all the groups are ready, say "Go" and the representative will join the group to the right of his own. The members of the group he has just joined will question him, in turn, asking *Yes/No questions* only, while trying to guess the object his group has selected. At this point the game is similar to *Twenty Questions*, (p. 65), except that there is no limit to the number of questions the students can ask.

The first group to guess the correct answer should raise their hands immediately. You will mark one point on the blackboard for that group. The representatives will return to their own group (those who have not had their object guessed will tell what it is) and another object and representative will be chosen.

The new representative goes to the next group and the procedure is once again repeated. The group that first scores five points wins the game.

# Neither Yes nor No

**Objective:** To provide practice in formulating *questions* with *tag endings*.

**Language level:** intermediate

In this game, one player is selected to be *It*, and answers questions put to him by the other students in the class. He must answer every question, but is not permitted to use the words *yes* and *no*. When he does so he is out of the game and the person who caused him to say *yes* or *no* takes his place.

The person asking the question must always do so with tag questions. For example: "You're an English student, aren't you?" "New York is a big city, isn't it?" "Jim is taller than Bill, isn't he?"

If he forgets and uses a direct question he is out of the game. It is important to keep the questions and answers moving quickly. The questioned person must not take time to consider his answers. A player is not allowed to answer, "I don't know," or "I can't tell you." A definite answer must be given and it can be anything the player wants to say—right or wrong—as long as it is neither *yes* nor *no*.

*A game might proceed as follows:*

**Student 1:** It's a nice day, isn't it?

**It:** A bit cloudy.

**Student 2:** But the sun is shining, isn't it?

**It:** Not too much.

**Student 3:** Do you like to sunbathe? (**S3** is out of the game for asking a direct question.)

**Student 4:** You like sunbathing, don't you?

**It:** I like sunbathing.

**Student 5:** You were sunbathing yesterday, weren't you?

**It:** Yes, I was. (*It* is out of the game for answering *yes*.)

# Thousand Dollars

**Objective:** To provide question and answer practice using the *future conditional*.
**Language level:** intermediate

This is a good game to play when the students are first learning the conditional tense.

One player starts the game by saying, "If I found a thousand dollars, I would buy. . . ." and then describes, without naming it, an object he would buy. The other students have to guess what it is, asking in turn, "Would you buy. . . . ?" The first player to guess the object correctly becomes *It*.

*Example:*

**It:** If I found a thousand dollars, I would buy something that moves along the road and has wheels.

**Player 1:** Would you buy an automobile?

**It:** No, I wouldn't.

**Player 2:** Would you buy a motorcycle?

**It:** No, I wouldn't.

**Player 3:** Would you buy a bicycle?

**It:** Yes, I would.

# News Reporter

**Objective:** To provide practice in forming *Wh-questions* and *Information questions*.
**Language level:** intermediate

A good news reporter asks five questions when he is covering the news: What? (or Who?) When? Where? How? Why? A lot of information can be acquired by asking these questions and that is why reporters ask them.

In this game the players ask the same questions that a news reporter would. One student is selected to be the reporter and leaves the room. The others in the class decide on a noun for him to guess, such as *pencil*.

When the reporter returns he begins his questioning.

> **Reporter:** *When* do you use it?
>
> **Player 1:** Almost any time.
>
> **Reporter:** *Where* do you use it?
>
> **Player 2:** On paper, usually.
>
> **Reporter:** *How* do you use it?
>
> **Player 3:** With my hand.
>
> **Reporter:** *Why* do you use it?
>
> **Player 4:** To communicate ideas.

The reporter continues asking the same questions but always gets different answers. These should be true responses, but not so obvious that they eliminate the challenge of guessing. When the reporter finally guesses the object another student takes his place and a new noun is chosen.

# Twenty Questions

**Objective:**   To provide practice in forming *Yes/No questions*.
**Language level:**   intermediate and advanced

Instruct each student to think of something that can be classified, in broad terms, as animal, mineral, or vegetable. One student is selected to be *It* and the others begin asking him questions to which he can answer either *yes* or *no*. The students must try to guess what *It* is within a twenty question limit. If the class cannot guess *It's* identity, the same person gets another turn to be *It*.

This game may be played in two ways. For intermediate groups, have each student ask one question of *It*, going around the classroom, in turn. For more advanced groups, each student may continue asking *It* questions, until he receives a *no* answer. A sample game might proceed as follows:

> **Student 1:**   Are you mineral?
> **It:**   No.
> **Student 2:**   Are you animal?
> **It:**   No.
> **Student 3:**   Then you are a vegetable.
> Are you something I can eat?
> **It:**   Yes.
> **Student 3:**   Are you eaten raw?
> **It:**   Yes.
> **Student 3:**   Do we also eat you cooked?
> **It:**   No.
> **Student 4:**   Do you grow on a tree?
> **It:**   Yes.
> **Student 4:**   Are you a fruit?
> **It:**   Yes.

**Student 4:**   Are you an apple?

**It:**   No.

**Student 5:**   Are you a pear?

**It:**   No.

**Student 6:**   Are you an orange?

**It:**   Yes.

The game is completed within the twenty question limit, and the student who has guessed correctly takes *It*'s place.

It should be made very clear that all living objects from the plant family are vegetable; all living objects which move are animal; all others are mineral. These categories include by-products as well. A wooden table, for example, would be vegetable. Human beings are animal. A typewriter is mineral.

Students should also be aware that they have only twenty questions and must be as economical as possible when forming questions. Once they have determined that an object is neither mineral, nor animal, it is unnecessary to ask, "Is it vegetable?" (See example sentence 3 above.) Many such questions can be saved with a little thought. You may wish to be flexible about the twenty question limit the first time the game is played.

# Secret Formula

**Objective:**   To provide practice in forming *Wh-questions* and *Information questions.*
**Language level:**   intermediate and advanced

One person is selected to be *It* and leaves the room. The secret formula is then explained to the rest of the class. Each student is to answer the questions asked by *It*, but he must respond *the way the person sitting on his left would answer.*

If, for example, Karen is sitting to the left of Tom, Tom must answer questions asked of him as truthfully as he can, but from Karen's point of view. If Tom is asked, "What is your favorite food?" he may answer, "Pizza," which is Karen's favorite, although he prefers hamburgers. For intermediate groups, the questions may be more obvious, such as:

> What color are your eyes?
> What book are you reading?
> How tall are you?

*It* may try to guess the secret formula at any time. Once every student in the class has had a turn to respond, the formula may be revealed, if it has not been guessed correctly. The game, of course, cannot be played in the same way again. However, it would be possible to use other secret formulas, such as the way in which the teacher would answer, or the way the person to the right of the speaker would answer.

# Where, When, and How?

**Objective:** To provide practice with *Wh-* and *Information questions* and responses.
**Language level:** intermediate

One student leaves the room and the rest of the class selects a word for him to guess. *It* returns and asks each student, in turn:

> "Where do you like it?"
> "When do you like it?"
> "How do you like it?"

Each student must answer all three questions before *It* moves on. The student whose answer reveals the chosen word is the next one to leave the room.

*Example:*

The chosen word is **coffee.**

**It:** (asking Student 1) Where do you like it?

**Student 1:** Almost any place.

**It:** When do you like it?

**Student 1:** Almost any time.

**It:** How do you like it?

**Student 1:** Hot.

**It:** (asking Student 2) Where do you like it?

**Student 2:** In a restaurant.

**It:** When do you like it?

**Student 2:** At the end of my meal.

**It:** How do you like it?

**Student 2:** In a cup.

**It:** Is it tea?

**Student 2:** No, it isn't.

**It:** (asking Student 3) Where do you like it?

**Student 3:** At home.

**It:** When do you like it?

**Student 3:** At breakfast.

**It:** How do you like it?

**Student 3:** With milk and sugar.

**It:** Is it coffee?

**Student 3:** Yes.

# Who Am I?

**Objective:**  To provide practice in forming *Yes/No questions.*
**Language level:**  intermediate and advanced
**Equipment and material:**  prepared name cards

This game requires advance preparation of large cards with the names of famous persons, living or dead, written on them. One of these is pinned to the back of each student in the class.

The students then try to discover their identity by asking, "Who am I?" questions to which only *yes* or *no* may be answered. The students should be allowed to wander freely around the room, asking each other questions such as:

> "Am I living?"
> "Am I in the movies?"
> "Was I famous for my beauty?"
> "Do you know me?"
> "Have I been in the news lately?"

The name on the card should be that of a person well-known to the class. Women do not necessarily have to have a woman's name, nor the men in the class a man's name, although that might be preferable.

When a student discovers his identity he sits down.

*Option:*  You may wish to divide the class into two teams, designated by red and blue cards. Students ask questions of opposite team members. The team with all its players seated first becomes the winning team.

# Questions Only, Please

**Objective:** To provide practice in *Wh-* and *Yes/No question* formation.

**Language level:** intermediate and advanced

This game can be fairly simple or quite complicated, depending on the players' ability in English.

The idea is for two players to carry on a conversation asking questions only. If one player forgets and makes a statement in answer to a question, he is out of the game. Of course, each player will try to ask a question for which it will be difficult to reply with another question.

In order that as many students as possible may participate at the same time, divide the class into two teams and place pairs of students around the classroom where they can speak without disturbing each other. You may wish to move about the room, making sure the students are playing the game correctly.

As soon as a student makes a statement he is out of the game and the other player wins that round. The winners of the first round can then play against each other for a second elimination. The game goes on this way until there are only two players left; the one who wins the final round is the winner of the day.

*Example:*

**Student 1:** What's your name?

**Student 2:** You want to know my name?

**Student 1:** Are you going to tell me?

**Student 2:** What will you do if I don't tell you?

**Student 1:** What do you think I will do?

**Student 2:** How should I know?

**Student 1:** Can't you guess?

**Student 2:** No, I can't.

(He loses the round because he responded with a statement.)

71

# Answer My Question

**Objective:** To provide practice in *Wh-question* formation with imaginative *responses*.
**Language level:** intermediate and advanced
**Equipment and material:** paper and pencil

Each student has two slips of paper. On the first slip a personal *Wh-question* is to be written and on the second slip two unrelated words. When the students have finished writing, collect the slips of paper and shuffle them, keeping the questions separate from the slips containing the two words.

After shuffling the slips, pass them out to the students again, making sure each student receives a question slip and one with the two words on it.

After the slips of paper have been given out, announce that the students will have two minutes in which to read them and write out an answer which contains the two words.

*Examples:*
**Question:** What are you going to do this evening?
(Based on the two words: *barber* and *ostrich*)
**Answer:** My wife and I are invited to a masquerade party; I'm going as a barber and she's going as an ostrich.

**Question:** Where do you keep your money?
(Based on the two words: *elephant* and *purple*)
**Answer:** I keep my money in a little bank that is in the shape of a purple elephant.

**Question:** When do you usually get up in the morning?
(Based on the two words: *angry* and *hot*)
**Answer:** When I get up in the morning depends upon how I feel; if I'm angry I try to sleep late, but if I'm hot I get up early and take a shower.

**Question:** How well do you play tennis?

(Based on the two words: *gorilla* and *tiger*)

**Answer:** Sometimes I play tennis quite well, like a tiger; at other times I play quite badly, like a gorilla.

# Nonsense

**Objective:** To recognize various *structural categories* and to provide examples within each one.
**Language level:** intermediate and advanced
**Equipment and material:** blackboard

This game is strictly for upper intermediate and advanced students, who are familiar with grammatical categories. On the blackboard the teacher writes the following:

1. an article
2. an adjective
3. a singular noun
4. an adverb telling *how*
5. a transitive verb
6. a cardinal number
7. another adjective
8. a plural noun

The students are seated in a row facing the blackboard. Following the instructions on the blackboard, student 1 whispers an article to the student on his right, who then whispers an adjective to the student on his right, and so on down the list and around the class. When each of the eight students has had a word whispered in his ear, he says the word he has heard aloud. The teacher writes the resulting sentence on the blackboard. It is usually, as the title of the game suggests, nonsense.

If there are enough students in the class to go through a second sentence, or even a third, a contest can be held to see which group comes up with the most original sentence.

*Example:*

| | |
|---|---|
| **Student 1:** | (whispering an article) A |
| **Student 2:** | (an adjective) beautiful |
| **Student 3:** | (a singular noun) elephant |
| **Student 4:** | (an adverb) quietly |
| **Student 5:** | (a transitive verb) ate |
| **Student 6:** | (a number) one hundred |
| **Student 7:** | (an adjective) fantastic |
| **Student 8:** | (a plural noun) bicycles |

The sentence that appears on the blackboard is: A beautiful elephant quietly ate one hundred fantastic bicycles.

# Tell the Truth

**Objective:** To provide practice in the use of *modals* in affirmative and negative statements.
**Language level:** intermediate and advanced
**Equipment and material:** A prepared list of questions; blackboard.

One student in the class volunteers to truthfully answer his classmates' questions. He is seated in a chair at the front of the room, facing the class.

On the blackboard the teacher writes the following model answers which the students are to use:

|  |  |
|---|---|
| I think he/she *does*. . . | I think he/she *will* . . . |
| *can* | *did* |
| *is* | *would* |

Before the "accused" is questioned, however, the teacher will go around the class asking previously prepared questions such as: "Do you think he/she is afraid of heights?" The student will answer either, "Yes, I think he is," or "No, I don't think he is," trying to give the answer he honestly believes is true. At the moment he voices his opinion he writes it down, along with the question.

After the teacher has gone all around the class (there should be one question for everybody and of course they should not be *too* personal), he will ask the "accused" to "tell the truth, the whole truth, and nothing but the truth."

It is now the moment of truth. The individual students ask the "accused" their question, the same one the teacher has asked their opinion of, and the person at the front of the room must answer truthfully, having agreed to do so. At the end, the class can compare their opinions with the true answer.

*Option:* A simpler way this game can be played is to have the teacher ask all the students the same question and have them write down their opinions, then ask the "accused" the truth and see how many came closest to having the true answers.

# Things Could Be Different

**Objective:** To provide practice with the *conditional* and *subjunctive* while stimulating group discussion.
**Language level:** advanced
**Equipment and material:** prepared slips of paper

This is a "What if . . ." type of game that offers practice with the conditional and subjunctive, using a series of prepared questions. Depending upon the language level of the group, you may give out prepared subjects on individual slips of paper for the students to take home and think about for the following class, or you may wish to announce one of the subjects and have the class, as a group, begin discussing it immediately.

The following ideas are suggestions for such a game and are useful for stimulating conversation.

1. What if Christopher Columbus had been lost at sea on his first voyage to the New World?
2. What if the wheel had not been discovered?
3. What if the ocean were filled with fresh water instead of salt water?
4. What if the airplane had not been invented?
5. What if the electric light had not been invented?
6. What if man could control the weather?
7. What if a new ice age should begin within the next five years?
8. What if everybody in the world spoke the same language?
9. What if signs of intelligent life are discovered on another planet?
10. What if science should discover a way to prolong life to 150 years?

# Turn Left, Turn Right

**Objective:** To provide students with an opportunity to follow explicit *directions* and *commands* using a physical action game.
**Language level:** elementary and intermediate
**Equipment and material:** a blindfold

One of the difficulties in learning a foreign language is to be able to understand directions when one is trying to find his way around in unknown territory. Asking questions is no problem because one can always plan ahead what he wants to say, but there is no assurance of what answer he will be given. This game is designed to give elementary and intermediate students practice in following directions.

This is a good game for a large room, although it can also be played outside, but wherever it is played there should be lots of obstacles. Assuming that in most cases it will be played inside, chairs and tables can be rearranged.

The person who is *It* leaves the room while the others rearrange the furniture. When they are ready they call *It*, who is now blindfolded, back into the room.

Standing just inside the door, he waits for directions. The other players, now lined up against one of the walls, have already agreed on a goal that he is to reach. In turn, each person tells him what to do, step by step. If he follows directions carefully, he should be at his destination by the time the final player has given his direction. He should *not* reach his goal before the last person has told him what to do, however. If this happens, the person responsible becomes *It*. Each player gives only one instruction: "Turn right," "Turn left," "Take two steps," etc.

If it appears that the blindfolded player is going to reach his destination before the last person gives his direction, instructions can lead him away from his goal momentarily.

When *It* finally reaches his destination (a chair should be placed there for him to sit in), he takes off the blindfold, gives it to the new *It*, and goes to the end of the line of other players.

# 4

## SPELLING GAMES

English being the diverse language that it is, spelling is often difficult for native speakers, and can be even more challenging to foreign students of the language.

The following games may ease this situation and hopefully in an enjoyable way.

Spelling Bee
Alphabet Race
Which Is Which?
Spy Code
Scrambled Words
The Alphabet Game
Initial Sentences
Ghosts
Alphabet with Doubles
Hidden Words

The Short and the
    Long of It
Geographical Spelling Bee
Spelling by Turns
T–I–O–N
Where Are the Vowels?
Telegrams
Word Chain
What's Wrong?

# Spelling Bee

**Objective:** To practice the correct pronunciation and spelling of a variety of vocabulary items.
**Language level:** all
**Equipment and material:** A prepared list of words.

An old-fashioned spelling bee has always been good entertainment as well as instructive.

Divide the class into two teams, and have them stand in lines facing each other on opposite sides of the room. The teacher stands at the front of the room, between the two teams, with a prepared list of words for them to spell.

The first person, often designated as the *captain* of the team, is given a word, which he or she repeats, spells, then repeats again. If the word is spelled correctly, the teacher then asks the captain of the opposing team to spell a word, and so on down the line, back and forth between the two teams.

When a word is misspelled the person who has made the error is eliminated from the bee and must take his seat. A member of the opposing team is then asked to spell the same word. This word, if it is an especially difficult one, can go back and forth between the teams several times until it is correctly spelled.

Fairly simple words should be used in the beginning, becoming increasingly difficult as the game proceeds. The final remaining student is the winner.

The students should be reminded that capital letters must be mentioned as such. With a proper noun, for example, if the student says, "b-r-a-z-i-l" it is an error; it should be *capital* "B-r-a-z-i-l."

Teachers should use their own judgment in choosing good words for their spelling bee. They should never expect students to know how to spell words that have not yet been learned in connection with their studies.

# Alphabet Race

**Objective:**   To practice spelling a variety of vocabulary items.
**Language level:**   all
**Equipment and material:**   Two identical sets of flash-cards with letters.

For this game two duplicate sets of cards will have to be made as there will be two teams and each team should have its own set. The cards should be approximately 5″ by 7″ in size, large enough to be seen across the room. The letters printed on them will depend on the words used in the game; thus, the list of words and the cards will have to be prepared in advance. There will have to be three *s*'s, for example, if one of the words to be spelled is *success*. There should be the same number of cards with exactly the same letters for each team.

The two teams stand at opposite ends of the room. When the teacher calls out a word, the players holding the letters needed to spell that word rush to the other end of the room and line up to form the word—correctly spelled, of course. Teammates not needed for that particular word may "coach" those who must spell it.

The first team to form the word correctly earns one point. Then the teams return to their own end of the room and wait for the teacher to call out the next word. The team with the most points at the end of the game is the winner. Only words the students are familiar with should be used for this game.

*Warning:*   This is a noisy game and should not be played where it might disturb other classes.

# Which Is Which?

**Objective:** To practice spelling a variety of common nouns, and to identify their relationship to a paired item, indicating same, different, or opposite.
**Language level:** all
**Equipment and material:** paper and pencil

There are two ways to play this game. If it is to be primarily a spelling game, then the students should copy the words that the teacher dictates to them; if it is to be a fast-moving vocabulary building game, they should not take the time to write.

Begin the game by reading a list of paired words. The students are to decide whether they are the *same, different,* or *opposite* in meaning. If they are the same the students write "S" on their papers; if they are different (but not opposite) the students write "D"; if they are opposite in meaning the students write "O."

*Example:*

| | 1. hot | cold | O | (opposite) |
|---|---|---|---|---|
| | 2. skill | dexterity | S | (same) |
| | 3. dawn | sunrise | D | (different) |

If this game is used for spelling, the list should not be so long, perhaps only 10 or 12 items. If it is for vocabulary building then it can be longer and move much more rapidly.

This is a good way to review recently acquired vocabulary and can be played at all levels.

*Sample lists of words:*
### Elementary Level

| O | hot | cold | S | large | big |
|---|---|---|---|---|---|
| O | above | under | D | brown | black |
| O | alive | dead | O | give | take |
| D | cup | glass | S | begin | start |
| O | always | never | D | breakfast | lunch |

83

## Intermediate Level

| | | | | | |
|---|---|---|---|---|---|
| O | poor | rich | D | ceiling | roof |
| D | brave | angry | S | postage | stamp |
| S | fall | autumn | D | shout | scold |
| O | ahead | behind | O | defeat | victory |
| O | borrow | lend | S | remain | stay |

## Advanced Level

| | | | | | |
|---|---|---|---|---|---|
| D | moderate | extreme | D | sweat | weep |
| S | prompt | punctual | O | tender | tough |
| O | moist | arid | S | research | investigation |
| D | shelter | cave | D | sting | itch |
| S | pursue | follow | S | wicked | evil |

# Spy Code

**Objective:** To review the letters of the alphabet and practice the formation of simple phrases and sentences.
**Language level:** all
**Equipment and material:** prepared messages

This is a good homework exercise and can be used at all levels, although each must have vocabulary items that are known to the students. The code is simple. The message is formed by putting numbers in place of the letters in the code. Different keys can be used but the following is typical:

| Code: | 1 | 2 | 3 | 4 | 5 | 6 | 7 | 8 | 9 | 10 | 11 | 12 | 13 |
|-------|---|---|---|---|---|---|---|---|---|----|----|----|----|
| **Represents:** | A | B | C | D | E | F | G | H | I | J | K | L | M |
| **Code:** | 14 | 15 | 16 | 17 | 18 | 19 | 20 | 21 | 22 | 23 | 24 | 25 | 26 |
| **Represents:** | N | O | P | Q | R | S | T | U | V | W | X | Y | Z |

*Message for elementary level:*

16–18–5–19–9–4–5–14–20    1–18–18–9–22–5–19    15–14
P   r   e   s   i   d   e   n   t        a   r   r   i   v   e   s        o   n

20–8–21–18–19–4–1–25
T   h   u   r   s   d a   y .

*Message for intermediate level:*

9–13–16–15–18–20–1–14–20    4–15–3–21–13–5–14–20–19
I   m   p   o   r   t   a   n   t        d   o   c   u   m   e   n   t   s

23–9–12–12    2–5    6–15–21–14–4    9–14
w   i   l   l        b   e        f   o   u   n   d        i   n

5–13–2–1–19–19–25
E   m   b   a   s   s   y .

85

*Message for advanced level:*

3–8–1–14–7–5    15–6    16–12–1–14–19
C h a n g e    o f    p l a n s.

1–7–5–14–20    23–8–15    23–1–19    20–15    8–1–22–5
A g e n t    w h o    w a s    t o    h a v e

4–15–14–5    10–15–2    8–1–19    2–5–5–14
d o n e    j o b    h a s    b e e n

5–12–9–13–9–14–1–20–5–4    23–1–9–20    6–15–18
e l i m i n a t e d.    W a i t    f o r

6–21–18–20–8–5–18    9–14–19–20–18–21–3–20–9–15–14–19
f u r t h e r    i n s t r u c t i o n s.

Another homework exercise, once the students have deciphered messages prepared by the teacher, would be to have the students devise their own coded messages for their classmates to figure out.

# Scrambled Words

**Objective:** To improve spelling by having students correct scrambled words.

**Language level:** elementary and intermediate

**Equipment and material:** A prepared list of scrambled words.

This is a spelling game in which the students are given lists of words, but with the letters scrambled. It is the job of the students to rearrange them. This could also be assigned as a homework exercise.

If the class has been working on a certain category of vocabulary items, such as food, furniture, or parts of the body, you may want to concentrate on this area for review purposes.

*Example:* Parts of the body.

| | | |
|---|---|---|
| 1. | KALEN | (ankle) |
| 2. | THRAE | (heart) |
| 3. | GIRENF | (finger) |
| 4. | STRIW | (wrist) |
| 5. | WOBLE | (elbow) |
| 6. | CHOMATS | (stomach) |
| 7. | RULEHODS | (shoulder) |
| 8. | WEREBOY | (eyebrow) |
| 9. | SITAW | (waist) |
| 10. | HODEFARE | (forehead) |

An extension of this is scrambled sentences in which the words are spelled correctly but are not in the correct order.

*Example:*

me the the in works shop girl for flower

The girl in the flower shop works for me.

# The Alphabet Game

**Objective:** To review the letters of the alphabet and provide vocabulary items defined by category and letter.
**Language level:** elementary and intermediate
**Equipment and material:** The 26 letters of the alphabet printed on separate cards.

Begin the game by showing the students the letters of the alphabet, though not in any special order. For elementary students it might be advisable to eliminate the more difficult letters, such as $Q$, $X$, and $Z$.

Tell the students that they are to concentrate on a specific category which you select: flowers, items from the supermarket, pieces of furniture, vegetables, clothing, etc. The selection of the category will depend upon the extent of the students' vocabulary and the categories they have been studying.

The playing begins when the teacher holds up a letter. The first student to call out the name of an item, in the selected category, beginning with that letter receives the letter. At the end of the game the student with the most cards is the winner. If more than one student calls out the same word at the same time the card is returned to the pack to be used later.

This can also be played as a team game, the team holding the most cards at the end being declared winner.

# Initial Sentences

**Objective:** To practice spelling and sentence formation.
**Language level:** intermediate
**Equipment and material:** pencil and paper

Each student makes up a sentence, the initial letters of each word, when joined, spelling a four or five letter word.

The teacher should allow a certain amount of time for the students to write down their words and sentences. When they have finished, each student should read aloud what he or she has written.

*Examples:*

| | |
|---|---|
| Peter ought to shave. | POTS |
| Ruth eats a lot. | REAL |
| Fred always makes errors. | FAME |
| Laura offered Cora a lemon. | LOCAL |

# Ghosts

**Objective:**  To provide spelling practice and vocabulary review.
**Language level:**  intermediate and advanced
**Equipment and material:**  dictionaries; blackboard

This is a good vocabulary game as well as one that gives spelling practice. Students may wish to have their dictionaries handy for this classic spelling game, although it is not absolutely necessary.

The students may be seated at their desks or in a semi-circle. The first student thinks of a word and calls out the first letter, which is then written on the blackboard. The next student calls out a second letter which will help build a word, that he, too, is thinking of, though not necessarily the same word as the first student. The teacher writes this letter next to the first one on the blackboard. Each student, thinking of a word, adds a letter to the ones on the blackboard; his word, of course, will be influenced by what has already been written on the board.

One important rule must be kept in mind as the word grows, however: the person adding the letter must make every effort not to complete the word. The minute he does so he becomes one-third of a ghost; three errors and he becomes a full ghost and is out of the game. The point of the game, then, is to add a letter to the word without completing it, although sometimes a student has no choice.

In *reputation*, for example, the word may build to r-e-p-u-t-a-t-i-o and the next student can do nothing but finish the word. There are other times, however, when a student unthinkingly finishes a word, as in the following example:

**Player 1:**  i (thinking of *interest*)
**Player 2:**  l (thinking of *illusion*)
**Player 3:**  l (thinking of *illustrate* but forgetting that *ill* is a word in itself)

The third player has unwittingly completed a word and therefore becomes one-third of a ghost. The fourth student begins a new word.

90

Each player must have a definite word in mind when he adds his letter; he cannot just add any letter he wishes. If, for some reason, other players suspect that he does not have a specific word in mind they may challenge him and he must tell them his word. If the word is in the dictionary the challenger loses a turn; if the word is not in the dictionary, the player who has added the last letter loses a turn. Neither one becomes a third of a ghost, though this could be made a rule of the game, if desired.

This is a difficult game and should be played only with upper intermediate or advanced students. To make the game more challenging to advanced level students, you may wish to set a minimum number of letters, four or five, for the completion of each word.

# Alphabet with Doubles

**Objective:** To provide practice in spelling words with double consonants or vowels, and to expand the student's vocabulary.
**Language level:** intermediate and advanced
**Equipment and material:** A prepared list of words; dictionaries.

This is a vocabulary building game as well as one which helps the students with their spelling.

The words defined below begin with each successive letter of the alphabet (except *X*) and contain double letters. You may wish to allow the students to use their dictionaries. This is also a good homework exercise. For advanced students, you may want to introduce more difficult words.

*Sample list:*

A __ e e ____   harmony; concord (agreement)

B _ t t __   a spread for bread (butter)

C __ s s ____   music of great composers (classical)

D _ s s _____   not satisfied (dissatisfied)

E s s _____   absolutely necessary (essential)

F _ d d __   violin (fiddle)

G _ l l __   four quarts of liquid (gallon)

H _ r r _   a great rush (hurry)

I m m ____   very large (immense)

J _ l l _   fruit preserve, marmalade (jelly)

K _ t t __   a young cat (kitten)

L _ l l ___   song with which to sing a baby to sleep (lullaby)

M _ n n __   way of doing something (manner)

N _ r r _____   a story (narrative)

O p p _____   a chance (opportunity)

P _ t t ___   a plan or model to follow (pattern)

Q __ z z __   several short tests (quizzes)

R _ d d _ _   a question that is puzzling, often misleading (riddle)

S _ g g _ _ _ _ _ _   one idea that may lead to another (suggestion)

T _ n n _ _   an underground passage (tunnel)

U t t _ _   pronounce, speak (utter)

V _ s s _ _   a ship (vessel)

W _ r r _ _ _   one experienced in battle (warrior)

Y _ l l _ _   a color (yellow)

Z _ p p _ _   a fastener, sometimes used instead of buttons (zipper)

# Hidden Words

**Objective:** To improve spelling and vocabulary by creating new words, using only a limited number of letters, derived from a single vocabulary item.
**Language level:** intermediate and advanced
**Equipment and material:** pencil and paper; blackboard

A time limit should be placed on this game, perhaps no more than six or seven minutes for advanced students and ten to twelve minutes for intermediate students.

Select a word that contains a variety of letters and write it on the blackboard. At the signal, "Begin," the students start writing down all the words they can find within that one word, using the same letters but in any order they choose.

For example, in the word *president* are hidden such words as: *resident, reside, side, dent, preside, net, ten, it, tin, desire*.

For intermediate students, words such as the one in the example are appropriate. For more advanced students, words with less commonly used letters might be tried.

*Variation:* As a variation for advanced students, instead of finding words within the word, the students can write down everything they associate with the word on the blackboard. With *president* they could list such words as *leader, politician, election, vote, voter, nomination,* and *campaign*.

# The Short and
# the Long of It

**Objective:** To improve spelling and expand vocabulary through a word-building exercise.
**Language level:** intermediate and advanced
**Equipment and material:** blackboard

The object of this game is to start with a single letter and add a letter to form a two-letter word; add another letter to form a three-letter word; and so on around the classroom.

*Example:*   Teacher writes the letter *O* on the blackboard.

| | | |
|---|---|---|
| **Student 1:** | adds *N* | O N |
| **Student 2:** | adds *T* | T O N |
| **Student 3:** | adds *E* | T O N E |
| **Student 4:** | adds *S* | S T O N E |

Going around the class each student adds a letter, altering the word to form a different one. The letters cannot be changed, once they are given, but the order can be. That is, the letter *A* can be added to *stone*, the *S* being placed after the *E* and the *A* taking the place of the *S*, forming the word *atones*.

The teacher, or a student assistant, writes on the blackboard whatever is dictated, the students first pronouncing, then spelling the word.

# Geographical Spelling Bee

**Objective:** To improve the student's knowledge and spelling of place names and geographical locations.
**Language level:** intermediate and advanced

As with a traditional spelling bee, the class is divided into two teams which stand in two lines facing each other on opposite sides of the room. This time, however, the teacher does not provide the words to be spelled. Instead, the first person of one team names a place and spells it. Then the first person of the other team names another place and spells it, and so on down the line. As these are all proper names, the students must be reminded that failure to capitalize the first letter of a name is an error and the student will be out of the game. As with a typical spelling bee, the last person left standing is the winner.

For advanced students, you may want to make the game more difficult by confining it to specific categories: countries, cities, mountains, rivers, or by restricting the geographical area to a particular continent.

# Spelling by Turns

**Objective:** To improve spelling.
**Language level:** intermediate and advanced

In this game the students are asked to spell a word aloud; each student, in turn, supplying one letter.

Begin by selecting a vocabulary item that is somewhat challenging to the students. Have the students, in turn, spell the item by providing one letter each. If a student provides the wrong letter he drops out of the game and the next student tries to give the correct one.

It would be advisable to prepare a list of vocabulary items, in advance, suited to the students' interests and language level. For intermediate groups, it would be useful to have one student write the letters on the blackboard as they are said aloud to eliminate confusion.

*Example:*

**Teacher:** Spell the word *station*.
**Student 1:** s
**Student 2:** t
**Student 3:** a
**Student 4:** s
**Teacher:** Incorrect. (Reads from blackboard: s-t-a . . .)
**Student 5:** t
**Teacher:** Correct.
**Student 6:** i
**Student 7:** o
**Student 8:** n

*Variation:* This game can also be played as a spelling bee by dividing the class into two teams, with each team spelling one word at a time. As an error is made the game switches to the other team. The team with the most completed words is the winner.

97

# T–I–O–N

**Objective:** To provide spelling practice using the *-tion* suffix.
**Language level:** intermediate and advanced
**Equipment and material:** A prepared list of statements, as suggested below.

This is a good game when working with affixes. It can be used as a homework assignment or as a short quiz of about ten items.

The idea is for the students to complete sentences with words that end in *-tion*. For example: Something that is asked is a ____ques____-*tion*. There are many other possibilities, using such prefixes and suffixes as *un-*, *-ment*, *dis-*, and *-ful*.

*Example:*

1. A club, company, or political party is a type of _____-tion. (organization)
2. When you want to be sure of having a room in a hotel you make a _____-tion. (reservation)
3. If you eat too much rich food you sometimes get _____-tion. (indigestion)
4. When you apply for a job you have to fill out an _____-tion. (application)
5. The opposition party led a _____-tion against the government. (revolution)
6. Every morning the weatherman makes a _____-tion for the day. (prediction)
7. A game that makes one think, such as chess, requires _____-tion. (concentration)
8. Sometimes when you are ill the doctor prescribes some kind of _____-tion. (medication)
9. A short pause while one is deciding what to do is called _____-tion. (hesitation)
10. When a crime has been committed the police have to make an _____-tion. (investigation)

# Where Are the Vowels?

**Objective:**  To provide spelling practice by having the students supply missing vowels from common vocabulary items.
**Language level:**  intermediate and advanced
**Equipment and material:**  A prepared list of words; blackboard.

In this game the teacher writes words on the blackboard but leaves out the vowels. The students must supply them.

This can be done in the form of a spelling bee, with two teams lined up on opposite sides of the room. The teacher writes the consonants of the word on the blackboard and the student whose turn it is must spell the word, putting the vowels in the right places. Thus, if the teacher writes *tlgrph* on the blackboard the student must spell out the word t–e–l–e–g–r–a–p–h. This may seem easy but the trick is that more difficult words are chosen for this game, although words within the vocabulary of the students.

Below is a list of appropriate words for this game.

| | | |
|---|---|---|
| description | pleasant | vigorous |
| barbarous | preparation | specimen |
| mathematics | ridiculous | persistent |
| repetition | definition | despair |
| business | propeller | personal |
| grammar | decision | continuous |
| gardener | loneliness | barometer |
| conquer | bulletin | |
| superintendent | prominent | |

# Telegrams

**Objective:** To provide practice in spelling and sentence formation.
**Language level:** advanced
**Equipment and material:** paper and pencil

For this game twelve letters are read aloud and the students write them down as dictated, putting six letters in 2 rows across the page, leaving enough space to fill in and complete words beginning with each of the letters. Two sentences that convey some sort of message, no matter how nonsensical, are thus formed. No more than five minutes should be given for the students to write their telegram.

*Example:*

P    R    O    A    N    P
H    F    S    W    S    Y

Please rush onions; Alice needs plenty.
Her father's supply was stolen yesterday.

# Word Chain

**Objective:** To provide spelling practice and vocabulary development through the use of alphabetically related items.
**Language level:** advanced
**Equipment and material:** paper and pencil

The first student calls out a word which he then writes down on paper. The person to his right must follow with another word beginning with the last letter of the word just named. Similarly, the third person produces a word beginning with the final letter of the second word, and so on around the class. It is a good idea for each student to write down the word he calls out.

When all the students have contributed one word the game continues on with the first player giving a word dependent on the last letter of the preceding word. The object of the game is for each student to try and repeat his original word in the second round of the word chain. The first person able to do so wins the game.

It is also important that students avoid words that will be helpful to their neighbor and all the more reason to write down his words as well as their own.

*Example:*

| | |
|---|---|
| **Player 1:** | Barn |
| **Player 2:** | Nose |
| **Player 3:** | Every |
| **Player 4:** | Youth |
| **Player 5:** | Hound |
| **Player 6:** | Drama |
| **Player 7:** | Airport |
| **Player 8:** | Truth |
| **Player 9:** | Hospital |
| **Player 10:** | Lesson |
| **Player 1:** | Noon |
| **Player 2:** | Nose (wins game) |

101

# What's Wrong?

**Objective:** To provide practice in recognizing spelling errors.
**Language level:** all
**Equipment and material:** Prepared paragraphs, duplicated in sufficient quantity for the entire class.

Divide the class into groups of no more than five or six students each. Give each student a folded copy of a paragraph. In the paragraph there will be 10 or 12 spelling errors, appropriate to the language level of the class.

Inform the students that they will find 10 (or 12) errors in the paragraph. At the signal, tell them to open the paper and, together as a group, find the spelling errors as rapidly as they can. The first group to find the total number of errors is to raise their hands, then the second, then the third. You will then check with each group to be sure they have found the right errors. The group to discover the 10 or 12 errors correctly is the winner.

As a follow-up, the class should correct the errors together as part of a whole class activity.

*Variation:* Other types of errors could also be used, such as structure or word order, for example.

# 5

# CONVERSATION GAMES

Many of the following games serve as *ice breakers* and provide a necessary step between controlled and free conversation, a major goal in language learning.

Don't You Remember?

Rumor

Out of the Hat

Continued Story

Serial Sentences

Famous Couples

Talking with a Purpose

Compliments and Insults

Cross Questions

Time Machine

Have You Noticed?

Crime Wave

The Mysterious Sentence

Let's Suppose

The Uninhabited Island

Tell Me Who I Am

Eloquence

Debates

# Don't You Remember?

**Objective:** To provide oral practice and reinforce vocabulary through the use of a fast-recall game.
**Language level:** all
**Equipment and material:** Slide projector and slides; or large wall charts; or poster-sized pictures.

---

This is a memory test and vocabulary building game, as well as a basis for controlled-to-free conversation.

Select special slides, or large wall charts (big enough to be seen well from the back of the room), and show them one at a time to the class but for only a few seconds. The slide or wall chart is then removed and the students are instructed to write down, or give orally, all the objects they can remember seeing in the picture. If there is a house in the picture, the students can include as separate items all the parts of the house—roof, windows, walls, etc.

The student with the most words wins the game.

*Variations:* One variation is to have the students write down only those words beginning with a certain letter. If there is a picture of a room, for example, the students, instructed to look for items beginning with the letter *C*, could write down *ceiling, carpet, chair,* and *couch*. Of course pictures with lots of objects should be chosen for this game.

Another variation is to ask the students specific questions about the picture. For example: "How many children are there in the picture?" "Where is the woman?" "What time is it?" "What is the man doing?" And so on.

See p. 8 for a written variation of this game.

# Rumor

**Objective:** To improve speaking and listening comprehension skills.

**Language level:** intermediate

Seat the students in a circle. Whisper a word or phrase in the first student's ear, but only once. He whispers what he thinks he heard in the ear of the student to his right. This student, in turn, whispers what he believes he heard to the third student and so on around the circle.

The students will hear the word or phrase only once and must pass on what they *think* they heard. The last student announces aloud what was repeated to him. You then provide the original message. There is often little connection between the original word and the one the last student speaks out loud. Sometimes it is fun to go around the class, once the game is finished, and have each student tell what he thought he had heard.

For more advanced groups, you may wish to provide full sentences for them to repeat.

# Out of the Hat

**Objective:**  To provide oral practice by having the students speak, without preparation, on a given subject.
**Language level:**  intermediate and advanced
**Equipment and material:**  prepared slips of paper

This game can be as simple or difficult as you wish to make it. Begin by placing a number of slips of paper in a hat or bag. On each will be written a subject, something appropriate to the level of the class. For intermediate students, it could be "My favorite hobby," "A trip I enjoyed," or "My plans for summer vacation." For advanced students, subjects may be more challenging, but should relate to topics with which they are familiar.

The student picks a slip out of the hat, looks at it for no more than ten seconds, then begins to talk about it. He does not prepare his talk ahead of time. He should talk for at least two minutes on the subject.

These talks could be recorded on tape and played back at a later time, or in individual student/teacher conferences.

A general question and answer period could follow the talks, but only after each student has spoken individually.

*Suggestion:*  It is advisable to wait to make corrections until the end of each talk. You might want to make notes as the students speak and refer to them later, but it is preferable not to interrupt the students while they are talking.

# Continued Story

**Objective:** To stimulate conversation through the use of an imaginative serial story.
**Language level:** advanced
**Equipment and material:** tape recorder

Begin the game by starting a story and continuing to talk for a short time, just enough to establish the scene, present the characters, and explain the situation. Then, just at a crucial point, select one of the students (or hand over the microphone, if recording), who must continue with the story from where you left off. Then, after a short period, again point to the next student who must take up the story from where the first student left off, and so on around the class, everybody contributing to the story in any way he likes without ending it; the last speaker is the only one privileged to do this.

After the story is finished, the tape, if one has been recorded, can be played back. In addition to being fun it also gives the students an opportunity to hear their errors in pronunciation, something you can point out once the tape is finished.

*Caution:* Some students are more imaginative than others and will go on indefinitely if not stopped, whereas others are unable to think of anything to say. It is advisable to stop the faster talkers after a reasonable length of time. When a student cannot think of anything to say, or very little, pass on to the following student, otherwise the story lags.

# Serial Sentences

**Objective:** To stimulate conversation by having students add a sentence to an imaginative serial story.
**Language level:** intermediate
**Equipment and material:** tape recorder

This is a variation on *Continued Story*, p. 108, adapted for an intermediate group.

The first player says one sentence, which is the beginning of a story. The next player, continuing from where the first player left off, adds a second sentence, the next a third sentence, and so on around the class. Each player will try to add a sentence which makes it difficult for the following player to keep the story going, not end it. When the game gets around to the first player he will add another sentence to keep the game going. And so on, until finally one unfortunate player cannot think of any way to keep the *serial* going and has no choice but to end it.

This is a good game to record on tape and play back for the class. Not only will it allow the students to hear their own pronunciation and intonation but it will also provide an enjoyable experience.

*Example:*

**Student 1:** It was a beautiful morning in June.
**Student 2:** "Let's go fishing," Tom said to his friend Bill.
**Student 3:** "Where shall we go?" asked Bill.
**Student 4:** Tom suggested that they go to Silver Lake.
**Student 5:** They got in their car and went to Silver Lake.
**Student 6:** For a long time they didn't catch any fish.
**Student 7:** Then suddenly they both caught a lot of fish.
**Student 8:** "We have enough fish, so let's go home," Bill said.
**Student 9:** So they started home.
**Student 10:** But on the way home the car suddenly broke down.
**Student 1:** At first they thought they were out of gas.
**Student 2:** So Tom went to find a gas station.

(And so on.)

# Famous Couples

**Objective:** To provide an opportunity for free conversation through a question and answer activity in which students seek to determine their unknown identity.
**Language level:** intermediate and advanced
**Equipment and material:** prepared name cards

In this game, there should be room for the students to move around, as at a reception.

The teacher will, beforehand, prepare large cards with the names of famous persons on them, each name one of a pair, such as Romeo and Juliet, Anthony and Cleopatra, Bonnie and Clyde, etc. There should be as many famous pairs as there are couples in the class, but only one name per card. Be sure they are well enough known that the students can identify them.

Fasten these cards to the backs of the students, who must then move around the room trying to find their partner. No one knows his own identity and is not permitted to ask, "Who am I?" He may, however, approach Cleopatra or Juliet and start a conversation in hopes of discovering whether she is his partner. He may ask such questions as, "Am I a character in a play?" "Am I still alive?" "Did I contribute anything to science?" and so on. As he asks his questions the person he talks to is just as eager to elicit answers to her own questions. Eventually, by questioning each other, the students find out who they are and who their partner is. Once a pair has discovered their identity they sit down.

*Option:* You may wish to divide the class into two teams before starting the game. The first team to have all its players seated is the winner. Of course, in this case, couples would have to be paired with team members.

110

# Talking with a Purpose

**Objective:** To provide an opportunity for free conversation based on an assigned subject.
**Language level:** intermediate and advanced
**Equipment and material:** prepared slips of paper

This can be a team game, with one representative of each team competing against the other. Only two players participate at a time, but the rest of the class will enjoy listening to their conversation while they wait their turn.

The first two students leave the room, and while they are outside, the rest of the class decides on two unrelated subjects which they are to talk about. The two students are called back into the room and the teacher tells each student what his subject is, either by whispering it or by writing it on a slip of paper.

The object of the game is for each player, in the course of the conversation, to introduce as quickly as possible the subject he has been given. Whoever does so first is the winner. The subject may not be forced into the conversation but must be used in a natural way.

When the students return to the room they are introduced to each other as though they were complete strangers, which makes it easier for them to ask each other questions.

*Example:*
**Student 1:** (whose subject is fried eggs) I'm very happy to meet you, Miss Alexander. I've heard so much about you from my cousin, Jenny Fisher.
**Student 2:** (whose subject is picture frames) Oh, is Jenny your cousin? She is a lovely person. We've been friends for a long time.
**Student 1:** Where did you meet?
**Student 2:** In school. I've known Jenny since we were in high school.

**Student 1:** She's my favorite cousin. I always laugh when I think of our childhood.

**Student 2:** Why do you laugh?

**Student 1:** As a child she loved eggs. In fact she wouldn't eat anything else. All she wanted for breakfast, lunch, and dinner were *fried eggs!*

**Student 1** has won by introducing his subject first. Now it is another couple's turn.

# Compliments and Insults

**Objective:** To provide oral practice and reinforce the use of adjectives in descriptive statements.
**Language level:** intermediate and advanced
**Equipment and material:** prepared questions

With a list of prepared questions the teacher, or one of the students, asks a question which begins with either: "Why do you like . . . ?" or "Why do you hate . . . ?" The question must concern an object or a person.

The first student replies, "Because . . ." supplying an adjective that begins with the letter A, the second student an adjective that begins with the letter B, and so on through the alphabet and around the classroom. The letters X and Z should be omitted. The game can be played with all students answering the same question, going through the alphabet, or with each student having a different question.

For advanced students the leader may prefer to call on students at random, thus making it impossible for the students to prepare their answers ahead of time.

*Example:*

**Teacher:** Why do you like Marion?
**Student 1:** Because she's attractive.
**Student 2:** Because she is bright.
**Student 3:** Because she is clever.
**Student 4:** Because she's diligent.

**Teacher:** Why do you hate Jim?
**Student 1:** Because he's awful.
**Student 2:** Because he's boastful.
**Student 3:** Because he is crafty.
**Student 4:** Because he is dishonest.

# Cross Questions

**Objective:** To provide question and answer practice using *Wh-* and *Information questions.*

**Language level:** intermediate and advanced

**Equipment and material:** prepared questions and answers

There are two teams for this game, each standing or seated, facing the other.

Each team has a leader. The leader of Team A passes down the line whispering a question (taken from a previously prepared list) to each member of his team. The leader of Team B passes down his line whispering an answer (also prepared beforehand) to each member of his team.

In making out the questions, and answers, the teacher should follow a pattern, such as: "Why does . . ."/"Because . . ." or "Where . . ."/"In . . ." Or "When . . ."/"At. . . ." Of course, the leader of Team A has no idea what the leader of Team B is whispering to his group, or vice versa.

When all members of both teams have been given their questions and answers, the first player of Team A will direct his question to his opposite number in Team B and the latter will give his answer, and so on down the line. The answers are often ridiculous, although they fit grammatically. If there is time for a second game, the two teams change sides, Team B asking the questions and Team A answering them.

*Example:*

**Team A, S1:** Why does gasoline cost so much these days?

**Team B, S1:** Because nothing in life is free.

**Team A, S2:** Why does the sun always rise in the east?

**Team B, S2:** Because what goes up must come down.

**Team A, S3:** Why does it take so long to weave a carpet?

**Team B, S3:** Because there are only twenty-four hours in a day.

*Option:*  For advanced classes, small groups or teams may write their own set of questions and answers, as long as they agree beforehand on the question and response pattern they wish to use.

# Time Machine

**Objective:** To stimulate discussion through the use of imaginative topics relating to famous people and events in history.
**Language level:** intermediate and advanced
**Equipment and material:** pencil and paper

Ask the students to suppose that, along with all the experiments in space these days, a mad scientist has invented a machine capable of taking us back to any time since the beginning of human civilization. Each of us can have ten wishes.

To get the most out of this game, assign the following directions as homework, and instruct the students to select one or two points to think about and be prepared to discuss in class the following day. Remind the students to consider the specific person or event they would choose, what they would say or do in that situation, and the possible outcome of such a meeting or adventure.

1. You may talk with one philosopher.
2. If a man, you may have a date with any woman in history; if a woman, you may have a date with any man.
3. You may take a trip with an explorer.
4. You may watch any one artist at work.
5. You may have a conversation with any writer.
6. You may witness a battle.
7. You may be present at any scientific discovery.
8. You may meet a famous ruler or head of state.
9. You may take part in one historical event.
10. You may visit any place in the world for one day.

Depending upon the discussion that is stimulated by each topic, this game can go on for some time, perhaps over a period of several classes. You may want to use one topic for each class lesson. It may be that certain other subjects, not included here, could substitute for those which may be less interesting to a particular class; with a class of young boys, for example, "You may meet a famous person from the sports world" would elicit a greater response.

These topics can also serve as motivation for composition assignments. The students would write down their choices and reasons for selection, as well as the discussion points mentioned above. Later, you could lead a discussion on the subject, asking individual students to read aloud what they have written.

# Have You Noticed?

**Objective:** To stimulate discussion through the use of provocative questions.
**Language level:** intermediate and advanced
**Equipment and material:** paper and pencil

There are certain things we see or do almost every day. However, when asked to do so we cannot always describe them.

Have the students take pencil and paper and write the answers to the following questions (or others that may occur to you as being better suited to your class). An interesting discussion should result.

1. What color is your toothbrush?
2. Do you put on your right or left shoe first?
3. Do you move your jaw when eating?
4. Which way do you flip the light switch when you turn it on?
5. Which way do you turn the doorknob when you open the door?
6. How many prongs does a fork have?
7. How many keys are there on a piano?
8. Are the buttons on your coat on the left or right side?
9. How many toes does a cat have on each paw?
10. When the water goes down the drain in the sink does it go clockwise or counterclockwise?

It is advisable to have pictures or the demonstrable means available to illustrate the correct answer, if there is one, and to resolve any disagreements.

For more advanced groups, you may ask them to think of their own questions, as part of a homework assignment, for presentation in class the following day.

# Crime Wave

**Objective:** To stimulate discussion through the use of problem-solving techniques related to an imaginative crime.
**Language level:** intermediate and advanced
**Equipment and material:** blackboard

This is a game that can be played on more than one occasion and become more enjoyable and instructive each time. As the students get more adept at playing it they themselves can make it more complex and thus more interesting.

The first time around, however, the teacher should take charge of the game, but later one of the students can take over, although a different one each time the game is played.

The teacher, without divulging any of the details to the class, chooses:

1. a victim
2. an assassin, thief, etc.
3. the place of the crime
4. a weapon
5. a motive: revenge, robbery, jealousy

The first time the game is played, items 1 and 2 should be confined to people in the class and the weapon an object in the classroom. It might be better to omit the motive until the students have played the game one or two times.

All questions are directed to the teacher, or whoever is in charge of the game, and must be *Yes/No questions* similar to those in *Twenty Questions*, (p. 65), beginning with general questions and narrowing down to more specific ones. The student must ask a general question to which he receives an affirmative reply before he earns the right to ask a more specific one.

119

*Example:*

| | |
|---|---|
| **General question:** | Is the weapon made of metal? |
| **Answer:** | Yes. |
| **Specific question:** | Is it a gun? |
| **Answer:** | Yes. |
| **General question:** | Is the victim a woman? |
| **Answer:** | Yes. |
| **Specific question:** | Is the victim the teacher? |

In the beginning, when the students have too little information to ask a specific question, they may wish to continue asking general questions until they receive a negative reply. Students should ask in turn, going around the class. They may ask about any of the categories at any time—victim, assassin, place of the crime, or weapon; however, the motive should not be discussed until after the other details are known.

If the teacher answers, "Yes" to a question, the same student may continue asking until he gets a "No" answer, at which time the next student gets his turn.

The game concludes when the assassin, kidnapper, thief, etc. has been discovered and his motive made known. This could be a team game with each side alternating questions; the winner is the team that guesses who committed the crime and why.

*Example:*

**Teacher:** An assassination has just taken place. It is your job to discover the following (writing on the blackboard): the victim, the assassin, the place of the crime, and the weapon that has been used. You may ask me any questions you like but they must be questions to which I can answer, "Yes" or "No." If I answer, "Yes" you may ask another question, but if I answer, "No," it is the next player's turn. You must ask general questions before you may ask specific ones. Let's begin.

**Student 1:** Is the victim a woman?

**Teacher:** Yes.

**Student 1:** Did the crime take place in this room?

**Teacher:** Yes.

**Student 1:** Is Helen the victim?

**Teacher:** No.

120

| | |
|---|---|
| **Student 2:** | Is the assassin a woman? |
| **Teacher:** | No. |
| **Student 3:** | Is the weapon in this room? |
| **Teacher:** | Yes. |
| **Student 3:** | Is it the letter opener on the desk? |
| **Teacher:** | No. |
| | (And so on.) |

# The Mysterious Sentence

**Objective:** To provide oral practice and encourage free conversation based on an assigned sentence.

**Language level:** intermediate and advanced

This is a team game with one member of each team leaving the room at the same time. The others in the class make up two rather ridiculous sentences and give one to each of the two students when they return. The object is for the two students to converse with each other and to use the sentences given to them in such a way that the other person will not be able to detect it.

The conversation should go on for no more than five minutes and when the time is up each player is asked if he has been able to detect the other's "mysterious sentence." He has to tell what he thinks it was, at least the general idea if not the exact words. A player gets two points for getting his sentence across undetected and one point for detecting his rival's statement.

The team with the most points at the end of the game wins.

*Example:*

**Student 1:**   (mysterious sentence) All triangles have three sides.

**Student 2:**   (mysterious sentence) My favorite dish is fried fish.

**Student 1:**   Good evening. How are you this evening?

**Student 2:**   Just fine. And how are you?

**Student 1:**   Very well, thanks. I've just come from Jack's house. I had to help him with his geometry lesson.

**Student 2:**   And I just came from Mary's house. I was invited to supper.

**Student 1:**   I'd rather do geometry than eat. I love geometry.

**Student 2:**   Really? I like geometry but not that much. I'd rather eat.

**Student 1:**   Well, of course we all have to eat but I am more interested in mathematics. Jack was doing some interesting problems with triangles.

**Student 2:**   Mary prepared a wonderful supper this evening. She's a very good cook.

**Student 1:**   Were you the only guest?

**Student 2:**   No, there were three of us, Mary, her roommate and me.

**Student 1:**   Was the table in the shape of a triangle?

**Student 2:**   A triangle?

**Student 1:**   Yes, a triangle has three sides. That would have been the right kind of table.

**Student 2:**   No, we sat at a round table.

**Student 1:**   What did you have to eat?

**Student 2:**   Fish. My favorite dish is fried fish, you know.

# Let's Suppose

---

**Objective:** To stimulate conversation through the use of hypothetical situations.
**Language level:** advanced

---

This is a game which is better assigned as homework for discussion at the next class meeting.

Either the teacher can give all the students the same topic for discussion or each student, or group of students, can select their own topic for presentation in front of the class. Instruct the students to consider the alternatives carefully, and remind them to jot down key words and expressions that will help them support their position.

There are, of course, no right or wrong answers to these questions which makes them useful for generating open discussion.

1. Someone has left you a million dollars. What are you going to do with it?

2. A scientist has discovered a drug which will cause you to forget everything that has happened to you. He has also discovered one which causes you to remember everything that ever happened to you. You must choose one of these two drugs. Which will it be?

3. A machine has been invented which will make you invisible for 48 hours. How do you want to spend these two days?

4. You can be any living person in the world. Who will it be, and why?

5. In the newspaper is a picture and story about someone wanted for a crime. This person resembles you, although, of course, it is not you. What are you going to do?

6. You have to make a decision about two jobs. One is exactly what you have wanted all your life; however, it doesn't pay a lot of money. The other job pays a very good salary but is not at all interesting to you. Which job will you choose and why?

7. Your car has broken down. You are in a jungle. You have not eaten for two days. Your foot is injured and it is difficult for you to walk. If you follow the road it will be at least two days before you reach civilization; if you take a shortcut through the jungle you will get to a village within less than a day. The jungle is full of wild animals. Should you stay on the road or go through the jungle?

# The Uninhabited Island

Objective: To stimulate open discussion by responding, either individually or in small groups, to an imaginative situation.
Language level: advanced
Equipment and material: pencil and paper

This is a good game to assign for homework as some preliminary thought should go into it. It also works well with small groups, prepared in class as an oral activity.

Instruct the students to take notes on the following information: You are on a ship in the South Pacific. The ship strikes a reef but does not sink immediately. Nearby is a small uninhabited island. You have a lifeboat and plan to go to the island. Before you leave the ship (which has everything you could possibly need aboard) you must fill the lifeboat with articles from the following categories. Choose carefully.

*Categories:*
5 books
3 movies (with a projector)
5 recorded musical compositions (with a record player)
3 musical instruments to play or learn to play
3 paintings
the equipment necessary for one hobby
2 changes of clothes other than the ones you are wearing
10 tools or utensils that are necessary for everyday living
7 items from a pharmacy
1 year's supply of food and drink
In addition, any three items not mentioned in the above categories.
(There will be a small battery-operated generator available for electricity.)

At the next meeting of the class the students will discuss their choices, giving good reasons for having selected them. If conducted as a small group activity, each group, or a spokesperson, presents its selection to the rest of the class. There are, of course, no right or wrong answers for these categories. A lively discussion should result.

# Tell Me Who I Am

**Objective:** To provide oral practice by having the students respond to information statements about a famous person.
**Language level:** advanced
**Equipment and material:** prepared situations

This game can be played in two ways, either with the teacher giving the facts and the students answering individually, or by dividing the class into two teams and having them quiz each other.

The teacher, or each team, has a list of 10 facts about a well-known personality. The first fact given is an obscure one. If the name of the famous person is guessed with only this one fact, ten points are received. If no one can guess who it is with this bit of information, a second fact is given. For this, nine points are received if guessed correctly. And so on, down to the tenth fact, for which only one point is received. The person, or team, with the most points at the end of the game wins.

If this is played as a team game, you may want to allow the two teams to work up their own lists of ten facts, and time will be needed to do this. It could be a homework assignment, each student responsible for ten facts about some famous person.

*Sample list of facts:*
10. This American contributed many useful things to the world.
 9. He died in 1931.
 8. Even as a boy he had an inventive nature.
 7. As a youth he worked as a telegrapher.
 6. He did much to improve the phonograph.
 5. Two movies were made about his life: one part as a boy, the other as a man.
 4. He had a lot to do with the incandescent light.
 3. He became deaf as a young man.

2. His name is associated with a place called Menlo Park, in California.

1. His first name is Thomas.

   *Answer:*   **Thomas A. Edison**

# Eloquence

**Objective:** To provide oral practice by speaking spontaneously on an assigned topic.
**Language level:** advanced
**Equipment and material:** prepared slips of paper

For this game a panel of four students is selected. This can be done by drawing lots. These students are the jury. The rest of the class is divided into two teams.

One member of each team comes to the front of the room. The teacher sends one of these two out of the room. The other picks a slip of paper out of a hat and immediately begins to talk on the subject he finds written there. He must talk for thirty seconds, no more, no less. The teacher, with a stopwatch, will stop him at the end of that time. He is sent out of the room and the other player takes his place, reading the same slip of paper and beginning to speak immediately on it. At the end of thirty seconds he, too, is stopped.

The jury then decides which of the two has spoken most eloquently on the subject, taking into account both students' ability to keep going, their inventiveness, use of vocabulary, pronunciation, etc. The speaker selected by the jury gets a point for his team. Then two others get up and choose another subject to speak on.

It may be advisable to list some appropriate vocabulary items on the paper slips taken from the hat, along with the subject to be discussed.

# Debates

**Objective:** To improve speaking and listening comprehension skills while stimulating discussion on a thought-provoking issue.
**Language level:** advanced

When the students' English seems sufficiently adequate, a simple debate is great fun and excellent practice, not only in the use of the language but in public speaking and debating procedures as well.

The teacher should clearly establish the rules of debating and choose from among the students someone to represent each side whose English is adequate for a debate on a simple, popular, and interesting subject. It should be something that can be argued without being too controversial. Local politics, for example, would certainly be interesting to the class but carries the danger that, in the heat of the argument, the students might lapse into their own language, thus defeating the purpose of a debate in English.

One student should be chosen to take the affirmative side of the question and another student the negative side. Each student should prepare his argument beforehand. This could be assigned as homework.

On the day of the debate each speaker gets up in front of the class and argues his point for a designated amount of time, probably three to five minutes would be appropriate. After each speaker has had his say, there should be time allowed for a short rebuttal. The rest of the class could act as judges for the debate indicating, by a show of hands, which argument was most persuasive.

Afterwards, if time allows, the discussion could be thrown open to the entire class.

*Some good topics for debate:*
Environment is more important than heredity.
There is too much violence on television today.
Examinations are unnecessary and should be eliminated.
Pollution is not as serious a problem as we are led to believe.
Childhood is definitely the happiest period in one's life.

# 6

# WRITING GAMES

Perhaps the most difficult of the four skills in learning a new language is writing. The following games offer practice in this skill, as well as enjoyment.

The Story of Your Life
Crazigrams
Short Story Nightmare
Predicaments
A Through Z
Analogies

# The Story
# of Your Life

**Objective:**  To provide written practice by constructing a serial story.
**Language level:**  intermediate and advanced
**Equipment and material:**  pencil and paper

In this activity, the students create several serial stories by following the teacher's oral commands.

Be sure each student has a clean piece of paper to start with, and then provide the following instructions by reading aloud to the class:

1. Write a boy's name with a brief description of him.
2. Write a girl's name with a brief description of her.
3. Tell where the two met and how.
4. What were his first words to her?
5. What was her reply?
6. What happened next?
7. What was the reaction of the people who knew them?
8. What was the result of all this?

After each command the student writes down the information that he has been asked to provide, folds the paper over to hide what he has written and passes it to the person on his right. The next command is given and the procedure repeated. There should be as many commands as there are students in a row or, if it is a small class, as many commands as there are students in the class.

When the papers have been passed completely around the class, the students open them and, in writing, join the fragments of information together with some kind of continuity. The resulting *Story of Your Life* is read aloud.

*Example:*
1. George Jones: tall and handsome, but shy
2. Louise Smith: beautiful, but very hot-tempered

3. On a bus: he stepped on her foot
4. Do you want to dance?
5. I'm hungry.
6. George invited Louise to supper.
7. Everybody was surprised.
8. They got married.

### Story of Your Life

Once upon a time there was a tall, handsome young man named George Jones. George was very shy. One day, on a bus, George stepped on the foot of a beautiful girl named Louise Smith. Louise had a hot temper and when George stepped on her foot she got very angry. George was so embarrassed that all he could say was, "Do you want to dance?" Louise was so surprised at this question that all she could say was, "I'm hungry."

They got off the bus and George invited her to supper. They became friends, much to the surprise of all the people who knew them, and not long after that they got married.

# Crazigrams

**Objective:** To provide written practice through the use of imaginative telegrams.
**Language level:** intermediate and advanced
**Equipment and material:** pencil and paper

Each student takes a piece of paper and writes ten letters on it—any ten, though without repetition—spacing them about one inch apart. He then passes the paper to the person on his right. Each student then writes a telegram, filling out the ten spaces with words beginning with the letters on the paper. An attempt should be made to make some sort of sense, although in most cases the results will be nonsensical. Thus, *crazigrams*.

*Example:*

M   R   U   L   A   F   T   B   S   H

Mary really understands Leonard's appetite. Fried turkey brings such happiness.

or

Mark ran uptown late again. Flat tire broke Sue's heart.

# Short Story Nightmare

**Objective:**  To provide written practice through a dictation and free writing activity.
**Language level:**  intermediate and advanced
**Equipment and material:**  pencil and paper

In this game the beginning of a story is dictated to the students, who must take it down, word for word. After the dictation, each student must add to the story, taking no more than two minutes to do so. When the time is up, he must fold the paper from the top, covering all that had been written thus far, except the last line, which remains exposed. Then he passes the paper to the student on his right.

This student, starting with the visible line, continues writing for two minutes, at which time the teacher will instruct the class to stop and pass their papers on. This continues until all the papers have been passed around the class and returned again to the student who first added his work to what the teacher had dictated. In a large class, several groups may be formed, perhaps by rows.

When all papers are back in the hands of their original owners each student will read his story aloud.

The part dictated by the teacher can be about any subject but should be interesting enough to stimulate the students to start writing immediately. A possible beginning might be: "It was a dark and stormy night. John was driving along a lonely country road when suddenly his car stopped. He did not know what to do. He got out of the car and began to go for help. Suddenly he saw a light in the distance."

# Predicaments

**Objective:** To provide written and oral practice through the creative use of hypothetical situations.
**Language level:** intermediate and advanced
**Equipment and material:** pencils and blank slips of paper

Each student is given two slips of blank paper. On one he writes a predicament. On the other he writes what he would do in such a predicament. Each student then passes his predicament slip two places to the right and his solution slip two places to the left. One player is then selected to read his new predicament and the player on his left reads the solution which has been given to him. This is continued around the room until each student and his neighbor have read their slips. If the students have been at all imaginative, the results are often hilarious.

*Example:*
**Predicament:** You are on your way to an important job interview when you slip and fall in the mud. There is no time to go home and change your clothes. You must be at the interview within the next five minutes.
**Solution:** I decide there is no sense worrying about it, so I just throw them into the nearest garbage can and leave.
**Predicament:** You make a date with Helen, forgetting you already have one for the same time with Alice. It is now 7:45. You are supposed to meet Helen at 8 on one side of town and Alice at 8 on the other side of town. Neither girl has a telephone.
**Solution:** Take a vacation at the seashore.

*Option:* For intermediate groups, you may wish to provide the predicaments and ask the students to provide only the solutions. The game then continues as described above.

# A Through Z

**Objective:** To provide written practice by constructing a short
  paragraph, using a different letter of the alphabet to begin each
  word.
**Language level:** advanced
**Equipment and material:** pencil and paper

Instruct the students to write a coherent passage of exactly 26
words, every word beginning with a different letter, A through Z,
though not necessarily in alphabetical order. It can be in any form,
including a dialog. Because X is a hard letter to find a word for, you
may substitute another letter. Other substitutions may also be de-
sirable, although for advanced classes this should not be necessary.

This could be a homework exercise which the students could read
aloud in class the following day.

*Example:*
  "Is Jim Evans coming to our party?"
  "No, he won't be able, for various reasons."
  "Does Marjorie's zealous uncle know?"
  "Yes, Xavier learned quite soon."
  "Good!"

# Analogies

**Objective:** To help students make comparisons in English.
**Language level:** intermediate and advanced
**Equipment and material:** A prepared list of analogies; pencil and paper.

---

In advance, prepare a list of analogies suitable to the language level of your class, with one word of the comparison missing in each sentence.

Hand out this list to each student, folded, and at the signal, "Go!" instruct them to open their papers and begin work. After approximately five minutes say, "Stop." Then go around the classroom and have the students read their analogies aloud.

The students with the most correct answers are the winners.

*Sample analogies:*
1. Feet are to shoes as hands are to _____. (gloves)
2. Author is to book as _____ is to picture. (artist)
3. London is to England as _____ is to the United States. (Washington, D.C.)
4. Black is to white as night is to _____. (day)
5. Ship is to sea as airplane is to _____. (sky)
6. Puppy is to dog as kitten is to _____. (cat)
7. Three o'clock is to six o'clock as _____ is to twelve o'clock. (nine o'clock)
8. Mexico is to a Mexican as _____ is to a Frenchman. (France)
9. A page is to a book as a room is to a _____. (house)
10. A niece is to an aunt as a_____ is to an uncle. (nephew)
11. Pig is to pork as cow is to _____. (beef)
12. Large is to small as _____ is to short. (long)
13. Hot is to warm as _____ is to cool. (cold)
14. Pretty is to woman as _____ is to man. (handsome)
15. Silence is to noise as listen is to _____. (speak)

141

# 7

## ROLE PLAY AND DRAMATICS

Some games lend themselves to the imaginative use of role play and dramatic techniques. These are often useful for generating free expression and the feeling of spontaneity in the language classroom.

Story in a Bag
Acting with Adverbs
Situations
Guess What I Do?
Murder
Charades

# Story in a Bag

**Objective:** To stimulate conversation through the inventive use of short, dramatic stories.

**Language level:** intermediate and advanced

**Equipment and material:** A variety of articles in a bag, one bag for each small group.

This is a story-telling game and offers a dramatic challenge to the class.

Divide the class into several groups of three or four students. Each group is given a bag containing five or six unrelated articles, such as a book, a knife, a bottle of medicine, an envelope, and a red handkerchief.

Team members have several minutes to invent a story that incorporates all of these items. Then each group tells its story to the class, using dialog, gestures, and pantomime if desired. The presentation should be as dramatic and entertaining as possible. Often a short play results.

With the intermediate level, you may want to allow more time to prepare the story, perhaps even give out the bags a day ahead of time and have the students invent their stories as a small group activity or as a homework assignment for presentation in class the following day.

145

# Acting with Adverbs

**Objective:** To practice and review the meaning of adverbs through the use of role play and pantomime.
**Language level:** intermediate

One of the students is selected to be *It* and leaves the room. The other students agree on an adverb. The teacher should suggest that they choose one that can be acted out without difficulty, such as *slowly*, rather than something like *lovingly*.

When *It* returns to the room he must try to guess the adverb by asking first one student, then another, preferably in turn, to act out the adverb in pantomime.

For example, he might say, "Eat in the manner of the adverb." If *slowly* is the chosen adverb, the student must pretend to eat slowly. *It* must ask each student to act out the adverb, either individually or as part of a group. If *It* fails to guess the adverb in the time set by the teacher, he has to give up. If he is successful in guessing the adverb, he sits down and another student takes his place.

*Suggested adverbs:*

| | |
|---|---|
| slowly | enthusiastically |
| quickly | fearfully |
| sadly | angrily |
| gladly | joyfully |
| tiredly | uncomfortably |

# Situations

<hr>

**Objective:** To provide an opportunity for free conversation based on an imaginative role play situation.
**Language level:** intermediate and advanced
**Equipment and material:** prepared slips of paper

<hr>

This game is best played in teams.

Prepare a variety of situations, perhaps in conjunction with situations recently studied, such as eating in a restaurant, visiting the doctor, etc. and write them on slips of paper, making numbered duplicate copies of each (two copies of situation 1, two of situation 2, and so on). Put them in a box, which is shaken so that the numbers get mixed up. Have each student pick a slip out of the box, and then look for the person with the same number.

When everyone has found his partner they sit down and look over the situation together and decide how they are going to act it out. The notes on the paper are only suggestions and the students should be encouraged to change them in any way they feel will be an improvement. After a period of time set by the teacher, the first team comes to the front of the room and acts out its situation, then the second, and so on.

At the end of the activity, the students vote on which pair has done the best job. It would also be a good idea for the teacher, at the end of the hour, to comment on some of the errors made.

*Sample situations:*

**Situation 1:** The scene is a restaurant. The customer comes in and sits down at a table. The waiter, or waitress, brings the menu. The customer looks at the various items on the menu and asks questions about each item, then rejects each one. Finally, after many questions, he leaves, saying he isn't hungry anyway.

**Situation 2:** The scene is the doctor's office. The doctor is seated at his desk when the patient comes in. The doctor asks the patient what is wrong with him and the patient replies, "Everything," and begins to enumerate his many aches and pains. The doctor listens, then says, "I think you should be in the hospital. I'm going to reserve a room for you right now." The patient says he can't go to the hospital because he leaves for a safari in Africa the next day. Perhaps when he returns.

**Situation 3:** The scene is a travel agency. The travel agent is seated at his desk. A customer comes in and says he wants to take an exotic trip. The agent begins to describe many possibilities. The customer asks about planes, hotels, sightseeing, etc. Finally, he says there is one problem: he has only $75 and wants something within that price range.

**Situation 4:** The scene is a hotel reservation counter. It is 11 p.m. A man/woman approaches the desk clerk and asks for a room. The clerk says there are no rooms. They argue. The person wanting a room insists there must be something; the clerk insists everything is taken.

**Situation 5:** The scene is a party. One of the guests is bored and wants to leave. He/she approaches the host/hostess and tries to make excuses. The host/hostess keeps insisting that he/she stay.

# Guess What I Do?

**Objective:** To provide practice in *Yes/No question* formation.
**Language level:** intermediate and advanced
**Equipment and material:** prepared flash cards;
  individual slips of paper

The teacher acts as leader in this game and selects three to five students to make up the *panel*. The others in the class participate as contestants, by asking, "Guess what I do?"

According to the level of the class, the teacher prepares, in advance, a list of professions for the contestants, written out on individual slips of paper for them to study. The panel must guess the contestants' professions using only *Yes/No questions*.

Everyone but the panel will learn the profession of the person being questioned, as the teacher, standing behind the panel, writes on the blackboard or holds up a sign indicating the student's profession.

The procedure is similar to *Twenty Questions* (p. 65). The members of the panel, in turn, ask the participant questions. Twenty questions are allowed, after which, if the panel has not guessed it, the participant reveals his profession.

For intermediate students the professions should not be difficult ones, but for advanced classes they can be more unusual and thus more interesting.

| *Sample Professions:* (for intermediate students) | *Sample Professions:* (for advanced students) |
|---|---|
| Mathematics teacher | Lion tamer in the circus |
| Carpenter | Political cartoonist |
| Auto mechanic | Concert violinist |
| Banker | Dress designer |
| Dentist | Window washer |
| Lawyer | Hotel manager |
| Barber | Gymnast |
| Actor/Actress | Veterinarian |

# Murder

**Objective:** To provide conversational practice focusing on *Yes/No questions* and *Information questions.*
**Language level:** intermediate and advanced
**Equipment and material:** prepared slips of paper

In setting up this game the teacher passes around a hat containing slips of paper. All of the slips are blank except three; two with *detective* written on them and one marked *murderer*. The two detectives identify themselves; the murderer, of course, says nothing. The detectives leave the room.

To do justice to this game the room should be completely darkened. However, that may not be possible, in which case a slight adjustment in the rules can be made, as discussed below. Chairs and desks should be pushed back as far as possible so that there is plenty of room to move around.

If the room can be darkened so that it is impossible to see, the lights will now be switched off and the players told to move slowly around the room. The murderer, moving among them, will tap one of them on the shoulder three times, thus *murdering* him/her. This person becomes the *victim,* and after counting to five (not too fast), he/she screams. The lights go on. The other players must all freeze in place. The detectives are called in and begin questioning the players (except for the victim, of course). They can ask any type of question they wish: *Yes/No questions* or *Wh- questions.* In order that neither detective dominate the situation, they should take turns questioning the suspects. Except for the murderer, each person should answer as truthfully as possible; the murderer is permitted to say anything he wants to. As the players will be stationed all about the room, there is no order which the detectives will follow in questioning them, and they can return to any one if they have further inquiries.

Now, if it is absolutely impossible to darken the room properly, instruct the players to move around the room until ordered to stop.

They should then be instructed to close their eyes until they hear a scream. The murderer, of course, is allowed to move among them and, as in the darkened room, tap the victim, who then counts to five and screams. The game then proceeds as previously described.

From the answers given, the detectives must try to deduce who the murderer is. When they are convinced that they know, one of them says, "I accuse you of murdering _____." If the accusation is correct, the murderer, for the first time, is required to tell the truth, and the detectives win the game. If, however, the wrong person is accused, the murderer reveals himself, and she/he wins.

# Charades

**Objective:** To identify words and phrases through the use of pantomime and spontaneous acting.
**Language level:** advanced
**Equipment and material:** individual slips of paper

*Charades* has many variations but all have one element in common: a player, without speaking, writing, touching, or pointing at an object, acts out a word, phrase, or idea for others to guess. This is best-suited for advanced classes. *Charades* is usually a team game and is more exciting if played that way, but it can be played with an individual student acting out a word or phrase for the entire class to guess.

If it is played as a team game, one group makes up words or phrases for the members of the other team to guess; there should be one assignment for each player, written out on a slip of paper. When it is his turn, a player takes one of the slips prepared by the opposing team, reads it and immediately begins acting it out. He is timed; three minutes is about average for each player. The other players on his team must try to guess what he is acting out. They must work as fast as they can because a timekeeper, with a stopwatch, will check how long it takes each player to act out his word or phrase. The team guessing the most words or phrases in the shortest time wins the game.

Signals are allowed, such as nodding the head for *yes* and shaking it for *no*. If a word is to be guessed, the player may hold up the number of fingers representing the syllables in the word. He may indicate whether a word is short or long by holding his hands close together or far apart. Many signals are permitted but they must be agreed upon before the game begins. Holding both hands together, palms up, for example, indicates a book, meaning that the title will be acted out. A movie can be pantomimed by pretending to grind the handle of a movie camera. A song title can be indicated by miming singing.

Each member of the team doing the guessing can shout out any word or phrase that comes to mind and should do so without waiting his turn. Time is of the essence in *Charades*.

*Example: (Gone With the Wind)*

**Player 1** begins by indicating that he is going to act out a movie title as well as the name of a book. He holds up four fingers, indicating that the title has four words. He then shows that he will act out the fourth word by counting to his fourth finger. He mimes blowing. Team members call out words until one says "wind," and the player nods his head in agreement. He then indicates he will act out the first word, and pretends he is going to leave the room. Eventually, his team guesses "gone," and the rest is easy: *Gone With the Wind*.

# APPENDIX

## Games by Language Level

| Game | Elementary | Intermediate | Advanced |
|---|:---:|:---:|:---:|
| I Packed My Bag for Alaska | X | X | X |
| Observe and Remember | X | X | X |
| What Do You Remember? | | X | X |
| The A to Z Banquet | X | X | X |
| Animal Squares | X | X | X |
| You'll Never Guess! | X | X | |
| Seasons Greetings | X | X | |
| Shopping Tour | | X | |
| Alphabet Identification | | X | |
| What's Your Hobby? | | X | |
| Color Call | | X | X |
| I Like My Friend | | X | X |
| Word Matching | | X | X |
| How's Your Vocabulary? | | X | X |
| Key Word | | X | X |
| Tessie Billings | | X | X |
| Vegetables and Things | | X | X |
| In the Dark | X | X | X |
| Teakettle | | X | X |
| Sally Smith | | X | X |
| Catalogs | | X | X |
| Words from Words | | X | X |
| Simple and Compound | | | X |
| Dictionary Dilemma | | | X |
| Name Game | | | X |
| Earth, Air, Fire, and Water | | | X |
| Buzz | X | X | |
| Buzz-Bizz | X | X | |
| Take a Number | X | X | X |

| Game | Elementary | Intermediate | Advanced |
|------|:----------:|:------------:|:--------:|
| Numbered Chairs | X | X | X |
| Numbers Quiz | | X | X |
| The Power of Concentration | | | X |
| Bananas | X | X | X |
| Big, Bigger, Biggest | X | | |
| This or That | X | X | |
| Roll the Blocks | X | | |
| Teapot | X | X | |
| Identification | X | X | |
| I'm Going to Take a Trip | | X | |
| First Guess | | X | |
| Neither Yes nor No | | X | |
| Thousand Dollars | | X | |
| News Reporter | | X | |
| Twenty Questions | | X | X |
| Secret Formula | | X | X |
| Where, When, and How? | | X | |
| Who Am I? | | X | X |
| Questions Only, Please | | X | X |
| Answer My Question | | X | X |
| Nonsense | | X | X |
| Tell the Truth | | X | X |
| Things Could Be Different | | | X |
| Turn Left, Turn Right | X | X | |
| Spelling Bee | X | X | X |
| Alphabet Race | X | X | X |
| Which Is Which? | X | X | X |
| Spy Code | X | X | X |
| Scrambled Words | X | X | |
| The Alphabet Game | X | X | |
| Initial Sentences | | X | |
| Ghosts | | X | X |
| Alphabet with Doubles | | X | X |
| Hidden Words | | X | X |
| The Short and the Long of It | | X | X |
| Geographical Spelling Bee | | X | X |
| Spelling by Turns | | X | X |
| T-I-O-N | | X | X |
| Where Are the Vowels? | | X | X |

| Game | Elementary | Intermediate | Advanced |
| --- | :---: | :---: | :---: |
| Telegrams | | | X |
| Word Chain | | | X |
| What's Wrong? | X | X | X |
| Don't You Remember? | X | X | X |
| Rumor | | X | |
| Out of the Hat | | X | X |
| Continued Story | | | X |
| Serial Sentences | | X | |
| Famous Couples | | X | X |
| Talking with a Purpose | | X | X |
| Compliments and Insults | | X | X |
| Cross Questions | | X | X |
| Time Machine | | X | X |
| Have You Noticed? | | X | X |
| Crime Wave | | X | X |
| The Mysterious Sentence | | X | X |
| Let's Suppose | | | X |
| The Uninhabited Island | | | X |
| Tell Me Who I Am | | | X |
| Eloquence | | | X |
| Debates | | | X |
| The Story of Your Life | | X | X |
| Crazigrams | | X | X |
| Short Story Nightmare | | X | X |
| Predicaments | | X | X |
| A Through Z | | | X |
| Analogies | | X | X |
| Story in a Bag | | X | X |
| Acting with Adverbs | | X | |
| Situations | | X | X |
| Guess What I Do? | | X | X |
| Murder | | X | X |
| Charades | | | X |

157

# Games for Children

| Game | Elementary | Intermediate | Advanced |
|---|:---:|:---:|:---:|
| A to Z Banquet, The | X | X | X |
| Acting with Adverbs | | X | |
| Alphabet Identification | | X | |
| Alphabet Race | X | X | X |
| Bananas | X | X | X |
| Big, Bigger, Biggest | X | | |
| Buzz | X | X | |
| Buzz-Bizz | X | X | |
| Color Call | | X | X |
| I Packed My Bag for Alaska | X | X | X |
| Identification | X | X | |
| In the Dark | X | X | X |
| Numbered Chairs | X | X | X |
| Observe and Remember | X | X | X |
| Roll the Blocks | X | | |
| Rumor | | X | |
| Scrambled Words | X | X | |
| Seasons Greetings | X | X | |
| Shopping Tour | | X | |
| Spy Code | X | X | X |
| This or That | X | X | |
| Turn Left, Turn Right | X | X | |
| What Do You Remember? | | X | X |
| Who Am I? | | X | X |

# Games for Homework

| Game | Elementary | Intermediate | Advanced |
|---|---|---|---|
| A Through Z | | | X |
| Alphabet with Doubles | | X | X |
| Animal Squares | X | X | X |
| Debates | | | X |
| Have You Noticed? | | X | X |
| Let's Suppose | | | X |
| Scrambled Words | X | X | |
| Spy Code | X | X | X |
| Story in a Bag | | X | X |
| Tell Me Who I Am | | | X |
| Things Could Be Different | | | X |
| Time Machine | | X | X |
| T-I-O-N | | X | X |
| Uninhabited Island, The | | | X |
| Vegetables and Things | | X | X |
| You'll Never Guess | X | X | |

# INDEX

161